YOU WANT TO
GO WHERE?

YOU WANT TO GO WHERE?

HOW TO GET SOMEONE TO PAY FOR THE TRIP OF YOUR DREAMS

Jeff Blumenfeld

SKYHORSE PUBLISHING

Skyhorse Publishing books may be purchased in bulk at special discounts for sales promotion, corporate gifts, fund-raising, or educational purposes. Special editions can also be created to specifications. For details, contact the Special Sales Department, Skyhorse Publishing, 555 Eighth Avenue, Suite 903, New York, NY 10018 or info@skyhorsepublishing.com.

skyhorsepublishing.com

10 9 8 7 6 5 4 3 2 1

Library of Congress Cataloging-in-Publication Data

Blumenfeld, Jeff.
You want to go where? : how to get someone to pay for the trip of your dreams/ Jeff Blumenfeld.
p. cm.
ISBN 978-1-60239-647-0
1. Adventure travel. 2. Voyages and travels. I. Title.
G516.B58 2009
910.4--dc22
2009008555

Printed in the United States of America

Dedicated to Joan, Julie, and Jenna,
and everyone else I've met along the way
who have made my life an extraordinary adventure.

Contents

ACKNOWLEDGMENTS

This expedition of mine into the adventurous world of book publishing was launched when Terry Whalin, my agent, met me at a conference in New York. He saw potential in recounting, from an insider's point of view, exactly what drives people to risk their lives in the name of exploration, and how their stories could inspire others who might want to undertake their own journeys some day. I've been an adventure marketing consultant for over twenty-five years; Terry showed me how to take a fresh look at these projects, and I am grateful for his sage advice and guidance.

Brando Skyhorse, my former editor at Skyhorse Publishing, assisted in further crafting this book to include advice for budding adventurers who always dreamed of a trip of their own, but perhaps currently lack competent outdoor skills or financial support.

A debt of gratitude goes as well to my editor, Abigail Gehring, who shepherded this project the entire way, driven by her own love of the outdoors.

Writing *You Want To Go Where?* has been a labor of love, for sure, one that has reacquainted me with the people who, since the early 1980s, have been such a major part of my career. I am particularly grateful to Jon Bowermaster, Dwight Collins, Jason Davis, Lonnie Dupre, Gunnar Marel Eggertsson, the late Ned Gillette, Mike Haugen, Carolyn Muegge-Vaughan, Paul Schurke, Will Steger, Reid Stowe, the late Colonel Norman D. Vaughan, Erik Weihenmayer, Gordon Wiltsie, and Robert Wells, among many others.

I'd also like to recognize Ruth Burton, a great friend who reviewed various chapters, whose resourcefulness on the Viking boat project I so much appreciated; Jennifer Kimball Gasperini, whose life was forever changed when she traveled north; and the employees of Blumenfeld and Associates who held down the fort while I was gallivanting around the globe on behalf of one explorer or another.

Richard Wiese, former president of The Explorers Club, provided valuable advice on the writing process, based upon his experience preparing his own book, *Born to Explore: How to Be a Backyard Adventurer* (HarperCollins, 2009).

Traveling a bit further in the Wayback Machine, credit is due to my first two newspaper editors: Madeline Conway of the *Evening News* in Monticello, New York, and Mike Greenstein of the Syracuse *New Times*, both of whom saw a spark of promise in a young cub reporter from the Catskills.

Finally, enormous thanks are in order to my clients, past and present. It's through their support that I've been fortunate to play a behind-the-scenes role in some of the world's most fascinating adventures and expeditions.

—Jeff Blumenfeld

INTRODUCTION

Five Simple Words

Perhaps Christopher Columbus started it all. Sure, there were some Vikings who discovered the New World, and Marco Polo's journey across Asia was a business trip well before he gained fame as a swimming pool game, but "adventure marketing" arguably started with the now-maligned Italian explorer who in fourteen hundred and ninety-two sailed the ocean blue.

While revisionists 500 years later charge that Columbus was simply a fortune hunter who left a legacy of exploitation and genocide, and there are some Icelanders—descendents of Leif Eriksson—who believe he was a latecomer to the adventure game, one thing Chris knew how to do was ask for money. So believes sports promoter Michael Aisner, who spoke at an International Events Group conference in Chicago.

Aisner pointed out that Columbus was getting desperate in his search for a fat sponsor for a high concept. Originally, he went to King John II of Portugal who took a pass after two reviews. Columbus repackaged his dream trip with a Spanish angle, but Queen Isabella I's review council turned thumbs down three times because pesos were tight—she was underwriting a nasty war against the Moors. But the Italian sailor was persistent. He found an agent who had contacts, and received an audience with the Queen.

Thus it was that adventure marketing was born—with Columbus, hat in hand, requesting funding from Spanish monarchs Ferdinand II and Isabella I.

"If we sponsor you on this quest of yours, what's in it for us?" they undoubtedly asked during the pitch meeting.

"I'll carry your flag to the New World and return with great riches," was the likely reply. Knowing he'd just keep shopping crowns, they put Chris on retainer for six years.

The rest is history. Columbus sailed. He delivered. He may not have been the first to discover America (it was already inhabited, thank you) but I'm thinking he must have retained a great publicist who carved an honored place in history for his ocean-going client with numerous cities, circles, World's Fairs, space shuttles, and universities named in his honor.

Today the spirit of Columbus lives on in the pitch letters, cold calls, faxes, and emails that pour into my office from an endless stream of dreamers, schemers, and legitimate adventurers and explorers who have their own high concepts but little means to personally fund them. They seek to gain fame and make it into the history books, or at least a yellow-bordered issue of *National Geographic*.

That's where I come in. I'm a public relations executive with an unusual specialty called "adventure marketing"—the business of connecting explorers and their projects with corporate sponsors looking to create awareness by demonstrating product performance in extreme conditions. Since my first adventure marketing promotion in 1982 for Du Pont, I've seen how a well-told, edge-of-your-seat adventure story can hold millions of Americans spellbound. Think of Sebastian Junger's fishing boat tragedy, *The Perfect Storm*, or Jon Krakauer's *Into Thin Air*, an account of a lethal storm on Mount Everest.

As the saying goes, "An adventure is simply a well-planned trip gone awry." For every scientifically valid, historically significant expedition, there are dozens of wannabe explorers circulating in the halls of potential corporate sponsors throughout the world. Nothing surprises me anymore.

Not the New York artist who wants to remain at sea continuously for three years without once coming to shore. Not even for resupply.

Not the Frenchman living in Texas who wants to swim the Pacific Ocean.

Not the eighty-eight-year-old man who wants to climb a mountain in Antarctica named after himself.

Not even the Minneapolis explorer determined to cross Antarctica—the long way—without using any form of motorized transport.

The challenge today is not so much to climb Mount Everest or explore the depths of the sea, but rather to figure out a way to pay for it all. There's an avalanche of proposals flooding into Fortune 500 marketing departments. Pity the poor brand manager who tries to pitch a Mount Everest expedition to management. Unless the CEO happens to be a climber, corporate decision-makers would rather be on the links than gasping for air at Everest base camp. Golf is well within their comfort zone—they can entertain clients in hospitality tents, run a sweepstakes for a day of golf caddied by Tiger Woods, or place banners that will be seen by millions of television viewers.

But sponsor a Mount Everest expedition? It takes a brave product manager willing to go to the mat on that one. Climbers can die. High winds can obliterate even the boldest, gaudiest logo printed in 48-point type. Or a blizzard could sweep in ferociously and suddenly create a life-threatening situation, as was the case on Mount Everest in 1996 when eight people died during a disastrous storm, prompting *Newsweek* to ask, "Are too many adventurers going where they don't belong?"

Sponsoring a risky expedition could be a product manager's career-defining moment, for sure. But planned correctly, with plenty of due diligence performed by the expedition leader and team, the payback can be immense.

The Coleman Company, which for over 100 years has manufactured camp stoves, lanterns, and coolers, signed up a Denver schoolteacher, a man who demonstrated he knew his way around a climbing harness and knew a thing or two about relating to kids. Not only did he climb Mount Everest in 2007, but he also participated in a rescue on the way down as he encouraged 7,000 schoolchildren to follow along online.

A successful adventure or expedition sponsorship can generate enormous awareness among a high demographic market interested in the outdoors, the environment, or physical fitness. The visibility is more focused than, say, becoming part of an alphabet soup of sponsors supporting a tennis championship or a marathon.

An extreme outdoor sponsorship can provide a halo around a brand. Send a sleeping bag to the top of Mount Everest and, assuming the explorer doesn't die from frostbite, this extraordinary use of the product speaks volumes about the brand, even if the typical consumer will travel no further than a Boy Scouts weekend at a nearby state park.

Evidence of the halo effect can be seen on those pesky hangtags dangling from outdoor parkas, sleeping bags, or backpacks lining the walls of Sports Authority, REI, and EMS stores. Buying outdoor gear and apparel "tough tested on Everest" attests to its durability. These tags scream, "Hey buddy, we could protect a climber on Mount Everest. Where are you taking your sorry self that's anywhere nearly as dangerous?"

―⌒―

Expeditions receive the most funding when the sponsor's product is an important part of the trip: products like Coleman tents, waterproof and breathable parkas containing Gore-Tex fabric, the latest Garmin GPS, and Vibram-soled boots. But there's another determining factor in whether an explorer will receive outside funding. I call it the "So what?" rule.

Sponsors want to know about firsts, because being first is newsworthy.

In other words, "Who cares?" Adventurers and explorers seeking funding have to go out and bite a dog.

"Dog bites man?" Ho hum.

"Man bites dog." Now there's something new.

"You want to go where? Climb Mount Everest?" the prospective sponsor might ask skeptically. "Excuse me, but I think it has been climbed."

Stacy Allison may have replied in 1988, "Yes, but never by an American woman."

Or Erik Weihenmayer of Colorado might have told his sponsor, the antihistamine Allegra, "Yes, Everest has been climbed, but never by someone who's blind."

Then there's Tom Whittaker of the Ester-C Everest Challenge '98. Whittaker took great pride in being the first disabled climber on Everest, summiting with an artificial right foot.

Imagine the pitch by expedition organizer Eric Simonson when he answered the "So what?" question sometime in the late 1990s: "Yes, Everest has been climbed, but we've yet to find the bodies of 1924 climbers George Mallory and Sandy Irvine."

News of the discovery of Mallory's body in 1999 netted worldwide exposure for Simonson's Mallory and Irvine Research Expedition.

Lately, more and more Everest climbers are slicing the "first" pie increasingly thin as sponsors become increasingly jaded. Two brothers from Locust Valley, New York, hope to someday become the first identical twin brothers to summit Everest at the same time. What's next? Triplets?

With all the hype heaped upon Everest, it is hard to believe there are actually tougher mountains in the world. K2, the world's second-tallest peak at 28,251 feet, is one that immediately comes to mind. Despite some cutting-edge climbs, highly technical new routes are on smaller peaks: " . . . the general public has never heard of Cholatse or Ama Dablam, and the American newspaper reader has eyes only for Everest," writes David Roberts in *Outside* magazine.

While prospective adventurers and explorers attempt to answer the "So what?" rule in one way or another, corporate funding is getting harder and harder to secure with the dearth of true firsts in exploration, tighter economic times, and fewer and fewer blank spaces on the planet—those areas of the world that were once unnamed and unmapped. Without a significant raison d'être, sponsors will most likely bury your request in their "Help Fund My Vacation" file.

Correctly answering the "So what?" question may well mean the difference between an expedition that captures the imagination of millions through the media, and one that trudges along in anonymity.

Simply put, newspaper, radio, and TV coverage means sponsor payback.

Erik Weihenmayer's Allegra patch is seen in *Time* magazine. Polar explorer Will Steger's Du Pont patch grabs valuable exposure for the company in *National Geographic* magazine. But those two, and others like them, came rather late to the expedition sponsorship game.

Supported by the National Geographic Society and some of the wealthiest men of his day, Admiral Robert E. Peary promised his North Pole expedition benefactors, "And if I win out in this work, the names of those who made the work possible will be kept through the coming centuries floating forever above the forgotten and submerged debris of our time and day. The one thing we remember about Ferdinand of Spain is that he sent Columbus to his life work."

When sponsors want to gain a finger hold in adventure marketing, they turn to their marketing consultants—public relations agencies, ad agencies, or the chairman's brother-in-law who may happen to own a backpack and some hiking boots. They also seek advice from one of three leading exploration organizations: The Explorers Club, the American Alpine Club, or the Royal Geographical Society. Sometimes they contact the agency I started in 1980.

Where did this journey of mine begin? How does one specialize in adventure marketing? For me, it took a long and winding road to arrive here. I was raised about ninety miles northwest of New York City in Monticello, the county seat of Sullivan County, New York. A small town of 5,000, it had very little going for it by the time I arrived in 1964, transplanted there by my father, a menswear retailer, who went into business for himself by purchasing a southern Catskills department store.

Monticello was the center of the so-called Borscht Belt, close to the predominantly Jewish resorts that lured city residents to the mountains for the cool air (a big plus in the days before residential air conditioning), and top-name entertainment from the likes of Danny Kaye, Milton Berle, Jerry Lewis, Don Rickles, and other greats of comedy. In fact, I worked with Milton Berle at the Concord Hotel. Indeed. He was on stage while I was waiting tables in the back row of the 3,000-seat Imperial Room, serving club soda with a "bissell of lime" to Yiddish-speaking senior citizens in wheelchairs.

While most people knew the area best for its resort hotels, that would change with the 1969 Woodstock Festival that roared into the county just ten miles away from my home. This hippie tsunami disrupted travel, overtaxed local services, and made a folk hero out of a local farmer named Max Yasgur, a customer of the Blumenfeld family business, who defied local authorities by allowing " . . . three days of fun and music," as he famously said during an address to the crowd.

Woodstock was a fun diversion, but what intrigued me most about my hometown area was a simple exhibit at the Sullivan County Historical Society that opened in 1974, dedicated to a local native, an infamous polar explorer named Dr. Frederick A. Cook (1865–1940).

The Frederick A. Cook Collection and exhibit in Hurleyville, New York, included a small video library and artifacts from Cook's various expeditions, including a polar sled made by his brother Theodore at their nearby homestead. A library of some 400 polar volumes, including many first editions owned by Cook, is also in the building. It was an early introduction to the rich history of exploration that would later form the basis of my career.

After studying TV and radio at Syracuse University, and a stint as a writer for two local newspapers (most memorable interview: screenwriter and *Twilight Zone* host Rod Serling), I entered the public relations field, eventually starting my own agency.

It was a long, hard road getting established, working at first for an eye doctor, a manufacturer of underwear for incontinent men, and an Eagle Clothes store in Ohio that scored a coup when it hired retired astronaut Buzz Aldrin for the store opening ("The Eagle Has Landed," said the ad campaign rather sheepishly).

Then came the call that would catapult my career. A client, the president of Cevas, a now-defunct ski-apparel manufacturer in Quechee, Vermont, asked that I contact Bob Bednar of the Du Pont Company to determine how Cevas could take advantage of the promotional money Du Pont might offer (Du Pont insulation and fabrics were major ingredients of Cevas cold-weather parkas and pants).

Bob, a lanky, fast-talking runner and tennis buff, soon took me under his wing. He became my mentor, despite the fact that he often took great glee in my personal lack of fashion sense. Going to work with one black shoe and one brown shoe, then on another occasion wearing a collar pin with a button-down collar (who knew?) are gaffs that Bob, now a jazz D.J. at a Jacksonville, Florida, radio station, razzes me about to this day.

Once my nose was under the Du Pont tent, and Bob introduced me to others; I learned about a Himalayan climber, John Roskelley of Spokane, Washington, who Du Pont sponsored. They turned to me for a strategic marketing plan that best maximized their sponsorship.

John had been retained to help Du Pont promote its new polyester sleeping bag insulation called Quallofil, said to be "the softest, most thermally efficient insulation ever produced from a Du Pont fiber."

The year was 1982, and John was best known for having climbed more Himalayan peaks than any other American at that point. He was also somewhat controversial, highly principled, and called a "staunch misogynist" in a profile by writer David Roberts for *Outside* magazine (which prompted me to jokingly suggest that John either buy up all the issues or hide the dictionaries from his wife Joyce).

Our fledgling public relations and events agency, just two years old by then, convinced Du Pont to host a luncheon in John's honor at New York's Lion's Rock, an Upper East Side eatery with a large thirty-foot-tall boulder in the backyard.

Invited were the top consumer and outdoor trade writers in New York. It was a home run. The restaurant overflowed with trade press from *DNR*, *Sporting Goods Business*, and *WWD*. Even consumer publications such as the *Christian Science Monitor*, *Field & Stream*, *Ski* and *Skiing* magazines, and the *New York Post* came to learn how Quallofil was "quallofied" to keep people warm. John was there to vouch for the product, while offering a personal account of the 1981 American Everest Expedition—the first attempt to climb Everest via the East Face.

It was the halo effect writ large. In fact, John claimed he could slip into a sleeping bag containing Quallofil, dressed in clothes still damp from a sweaty day of climbing, and wake up warm and dry the next morning. I couldn't have scripted it better myself.

Later, in a shameless bit of puffery, we had John attend the national Boy Scout Jamboree to run a sleeping bag stuffing contest called "Huff, Puff, and Stuff" to demonstrate how well Quallofil would compact into stuff sacks. Over 500 Scouts and their leaders participated, much to our delight.

The success of these two events led to more work with Du Pont until the company comprised 80 percent of our business. It was a financially dangerous, overly dependent position to be in, but the money was hard to resist.

Within a short time, we were reviewing hundreds of adventure sponsorship requests, while selecting only a few for implementation. Our staff was organizing press conferences, luncheons, trade show appearances, and speaking engagements. We sent an account executive to staff a remote base station in the High Arctic; convinced ski instructors in the Andes to test a new type of thermal underwear; and once took reporters on a climb up Mount Washington, New Hampshire, home of the world's worst weather and site of the highest recorded surface wind on earth.

Our reputation grew, and we became inundated with sponsorship requests we knew Du Pont would never accept. One day it dawned on us to create a list of available sponsorships that Du Pont previously declined, a list we could share with other potential corporate sponsors.

This led to the creation of *Expedition News* in October 1994—initially just a fax that we sent out to dozens of potential sponsors, hoping they would, in turn, hire Blumenfeld and Associates to plan and implement their own adventure marketing programs.

The fax led to an early form of an email newsletter sent, somewhat awkwardly, via MCI Mail. *Expedition News* then morphed into a printed publication distributed to hundreds at a subscription cost of $36 per year. Today *EN* is back to email distribution, is excerpted in The Explorers Club's *Explorers Journal,* and is available on the Web (expeditionnews .com) for the estimated 10,000 who read it monthly.

The Web is packed with obscure advice. There are over 1,300 *Dummies* books covering everything from dating to low-fat cooking to beagles. Most people, as part of their everyday lives, can seek advice from accountants, lawyers, doctors, clergymen, and financial planners. But where do you turn for advice on how to raise $100,000 for an expedition to discover the sea serpent said to live between New York and Vermont in Lake Champlain? Or what if you need a sponsor to help you blog your way from New York City to Ushuaia, Argentina, the southernmost city in the world?

That's where this book comes in. Within the following pages I'll take you from the North Pole to the South Pole, from the tallest peak in the world to the lowest point in North America, and across and under the seas. You'll learn from some of the most famous explorers of the eighteenth, nineteenth, and twentieth centuries, plus a few in the twenty-first now slogging their way into the record books.

Despite the late Colonel Norman D. Vaughan's ambitious and endearing plan to climb a mountain in Antarctica named after himself, the sponsorship search was hardly easy for the octogenarian. It wasn't smooth sailing either for New Yorker Reid Stowe who scrounged enough funds to eventually attempt history's longest continuous sea voyage. How was

Minnesotan Will Steger able to convince W. L. Gore & Associates and the French insurance company UAP to each pony up $2 million to sponsor the first dogsled traverse of Antarctica? A master at obtaining sponsorship, Will admitted to Mike Cannell of the *New York Times* during the planning of his $11 million Trans-Antarctica Expedition, "The biggest struggle is behind the scenes. It's not just a question of whether I can ski thirty miles in one day, but can I actually raise the money and get this thing organized?"

In the following pages I'll explain how many of the adventure world's most famous boldface names humbly took hat in hand, traveled to attend pitch meetings with potential sponsors, and attempted to sell their dream of adventure and exploration. You'll learn how they raised the funds they needed and how you can as well.

Then I'll explain not only what to do with the funding before, during, and after your project, but even suggest a few adventures and expeditions to consider launching on your own.

This is the story of dedicated individuals who have expanded our understanding of the earth and the limits of human performance. It's the story of extraordinary adventurers and explorers who have enriched our lives through their tales of perseverance despite incredible odds.

$$\text{\Large ☂}$$

Usually my first conversation with these brave, if ofttimes eccentric, individuals begins with five simple words:

You want to go where?

YOU WANT TO GO WHERE?

THE "SO WHAT?" RULE

This book makes a careful distinction between adventures and expeditions, and it's important to understand the difference between the two. An expedition is a journey that involves scientific study or field research—an effort to better understand the planet, determine what lies over the next hill, or test the upper limits of human performance, whether that entails jumping from the edge of space, diving 560 feet on a single breath of air, or climbing Mount Everest without oxygen. In short, it's a trip with a purpose.

A visit to Iceland to enjoy hiking, soak in hot tubs, and pursue members of the opposite sex in some famed Reykjavik nightclub is clearly a vacation. But travel to that same island nation in the North Atlantic, arrive as a citizen scientist to help uncover homes covered in ash during a 1973 volcanic eruption, and then write a magazine article or lecture about it, and you've got yourself an expedition.

An adventure, on the other hand, is a trip with, say, a potentially unexpected or unwanted outcome. It involves an unusual and exciting, typically hazardous experience or activity. Or to put it another way, an adventure is often what happens when you make a mistake. According to the late adventurer Edward "Ned" Gillette in an *Outside* magazine interview, "Adventure is looking at old subjects in new ways. None of us are explorers anymore. We're guys who dream up things that might be fun to do."

Sponsors are called upon to constantly make the distinction between an adventure, an expedition, or simply someone's fun time in the great outdoors.

Time magazine's John Skow referred to this search for other people's money as a process whereby " . . . idlers with powerful legs try to persuade achievers in powerful suits to pay for their vacations."

Du Pont executive Felix P. Connolly's interview in *Adweek* magazine years ago still holds true for many corporate sponsors besieged by requests: "We turn down ninety-nine percent of them. It seems every college kid who ever climbed a mountain and decides that he'll assault Everest before settling down calls us."

Is sponsorship funding available for projects that answer the "So what?" question? Yes. Is it easy to secure such funding? Not in the least. But it is possible, as I am about to explain.

$$\textbf{\textit{?}}$$

The phone rings one day in the fall of 2008. It's a cold call, and I could sense it was going to be another one of those "You want to go where?" moments. On the line was Len Waldron, the vice president of a major financial services company just outside Manhattan. That's his day job. In his spare time Len, a former U.S. Army infantry officer in his mid-thirties, likes to write about fishing for enthusiast magazines such as *Destination Fish* and *Flyfishing & Tying Journal*.

For months, he had been percolating an idea for a fishing adventure, one that he hoped someone else would help fund. As an avid fly fisherman, I was immediately intrigued. I've been on a number of fly-fishing adventures myself, personally paying for them all, right down to the very last wooly bugger. These were fun vacations. What I lacked was an angle, a "hook" if you will, something to help the project stand apart.

"You're going on a fishing adventure? So what?" a potential sponsor might say. "How will that help our company move the needle?"

Anticipating this kind of corporate pushback, Len told me he worked hard to develop the adventure's raison d'être. After much research and numerous conversations with conservationists, he would dedicate his trip to the roadless and wild areas of the Pacific Northwest, urging balanced use and conservation of what he calls "one of the continent's greatest natural resources."

To make the project even more compelling, he would hire a pilot to fly a film crew and himself to remote fishing lakes in a refurbished Grumman G-21 "Goose" amphibian airplane, originally built by Grumman Aircraft in 1936. It's the ATV of the land, sea, and air, able to take off and land on paved runways, dirt strips, grass strips, and in water as shallow as three feet.

When you take an accomplished freelance writer, a worthy cause, and combine it with an aircraft that looks like it flew out of the pages of a Dashiell Hammett novel, then wrap it into a proposal that promises magazine publicity, photography, video, and daily blogs, it becomes an almost irresistible package. He was targeting adventure clothing manufacturers, liquor companies that use geese in their name and logo, and other categories—digital cameras, footwear, GPS navigation systems, and major outdoor retail chains.

Len is already thinking beyond his Goose project, to another adventure, this one in the Patagonia region of South America. Still in the planning stages, that project is timed to coincide with the emergence of a big, nasty beetle called the catabria, often likened to fishing with a porterhouse steak. Monstrous brown trout eat it like candy, providing the kind of "hero" images sure to lure readers of fishing magazines.

Now let's say you're an avid golfer. You dream about the sport. You read golf magazines, own a collection of inane Tim Conway *Dorf on Golf* videos, and have a mounted-golf-ball clock in the office right above the little carpet putting green you bought for yourself.

Travel to Myrtle Beach for the weekend and we'd call that a vacation. But what if you combined a passion for golf with a love of adventure? An adventure like hitting a golf ball across Mongolia, the small Asian nation landlocked between China and Russia? The lads back at the club will seethe with jealously when you return with stories of using a three-iron to hit hundreds of golf balls across the treeless steppes. Explain that someone else paid for at least part of the trip, and your green-panted buddies will likely become speechless, practically incontinent.

Sound far-fetched? Well, that's exactly what an American civil engineer in his early thirties named Andre Tolme accomplished during the summers of 2003 and 2004.

Andre came up with a simple title, "Golf Mongolia," established a Web site, and contacted corporate sponsors for in-kind and cash donations. Sierra Designs, the Colorado Yurt Company, and the Neighborhood Mortgage Company all came aboard, along with many friends, family, and international admirers who sponsored balls for $25 to $50. Out of a total shoestring budget of $4,000, including airfare, he raised about 50 percent through cash and in-kind support.

To reach the first "tee," Andre took a train north from Beijing to Ulan Bator, then bused to the eastern city of Choybalsan. From there, he spent five months, hitting 420 golf balls 2.322 million yards (1,319 miles)—a par 11,880—until he reached the western city of Khovd.

A resident of Berkeley, California, Andre decided "winter rules" would apply—he allowed himself the luxury of taking a preferred lie within one club length of where the ball lands. He said, "This avoided having to hit every shot from the rough, which would be tedious and uninteresting."

Still, like all good adventures, the ninety-day project wasn't entirely risk-free. He had to contend with 509 lost balls, hitting into hazards, a harsh climate, marmots carrying bubonic plague, and four species of poisonous snakes that could strike at any time. Not to mention a diet of mutton fat, fermented horse milk, and schmears of sheep brain on slices of sheep's liver.

He blogged, "Some may call this extreme golf, adventure expression, or just plain crazy. One thing is certain, this has never been done before and may never be done again."

Various national media apparently agreed. Andre appeared on *The Tonight Show, The Today Show, CNN,* and conducted numerous newspaper interviews. "You hit the ball, then you go and find it. Then you hit it again," he told the *New York Times'* Dave Anderson, who called him "Golfer of the Year."

A guest appearance with Jay Leno became an opportunity to confess he was "independently poor" and was looking for sponsors for his next adventure, which Andre explains might be in North Africa where he expects to encounter the world's largest sand trap.

Andre's adventure in extreme golf provides hope for all of us who want to convince someone to pay for a trip, but find an expedition to Everest base camp, Kilimanjaro, or the North Pole somewhat daunting. Truth be told, "Golfing Mongolia" is a great adventure, but an expedition it's not. No field research, no scientific studies, just a great story to tell. Which is fine. It abides by the "So what?" rule. You're not just traveling to Mongolia, you're accomplishing a feat of endurance. It was a simple idea executed flawlessly.

Clearly, less is more when you're trying to raise funds for an expedition. The explorer H. W. "Bill" Tilman (1898–1977) is famously credited with saying, "Any worthwhile expedition can be planned on the back of an envelope."

In the late 1980s one adventure came along that could be summarized on the back of a postage stamp. It passed the "So what?" test with flying colors, and it began with one of those "cold calls." I lifted the telephone receiver one day in 1987, and there on the line boomed a voice with a slight Boston accent cracked with age. "Mr. Blumenfeld, I want to climb a mountain in Antarctica." As I girded myself for yet another desperate but mundane pitch, the caller continued, "It's not the highest mountain in Antarctica. It's not even the most remote. But it is named after me."

I thought to myself, "How'd that happen?" How do you have a mountain named after yourself in the coldest, highest, windiest continent on earth? There's a town in Germany named "Blumenfeld," and a bad Welsh spy movie named *Operation Blumenfeld.* I give Blumenfeld extra virgin olive oil from New Zealand as Christmas gifts. So if they're handing out mountains, I'm in.

But being honored with a namesake mountain in Antarctica takes some doing. One way, as I soon learned, is to be the last surviving member of Admiral Richard E. Byrd's 1928–1930 expedition. War hero, dogsled competitor, and big-time dreamer, the late Colonel Norman D. Vaughan, age eighty-two at the time, was on the phone and needed sponsorship assistance from my clients.

Norman, a native of Salem, Massachusetts, was the last living link to the early twentieth century's rich history of polar discovery, and Admiral Byrd himself honored Norman by naming a 10,302-foot peak located 450 miles inland in the Queen Maud Range "Mount Vaughan."

Later, Norman would go on to compete in the 1932 Olympics as a dogsled musher where he would finish tenth in the only year that dogsledding was allowed as a demonstration sport. During World War II, he commanded 425 dogs as part of U.S. Army Air Corps Search and Rescue, and retrieved top-secret WWII Norden bombsights before German submarine crews could reach the Lost Squadron—two fuel-starved B-17s that were forced to land in Greenland due to bad weather. Norman was a competitor in thirteen Iditarod sled dog races, competing in the approximately 1,150-mile race as recently as 1992 at age eighty-six.

An attempt at a first ascent of his namesake mountain failed on November 26, 1993, when the expedition's DC-6 supply plane, its airborne freight horse, crashed due to poor visibility on Antarctica, six miles from the Patriot Hills blue-ice airstrip. They were descending through the clouds when suddenly the plane hit the deck unexpectedly. The pilot had literally flown into the ground. Landing gears were ripped off and strewn behind them, according to an expedition update sent to friends, the media, and sponsors. Three props came spinning off. Everyone was thrown forward.

The accident severely injured team veterinarian Dr. Jerry Vanek, a University of Minnesota professor, when his airplane seat broke loose from its footing and slammed into the bulkhead. He wound up on the floor on his back, legs over the top of him, still belted in his seat. Vanek suffered a fractured skull, deep facial lacerations, and puncture wounds on the head, as well as multiple leg and arm fractures. He would eventually recover, thanks to a medical evacuation by a C-130 Hercules to Punta Arenas, Chile, privately financed by the Antarctic aviation company, Adventure Network International.

Norman would relive that moment in a memo to my staff: "When the plane crashed, the dogs were quickly tossed off the plane because there was fuel spilling everywhere, and one engine was on fire. Once off the plane, our handler, Larry Grout, put them all on picket lines staked to the debris. However, a fuel line broke with more gas pouring down to exactly where the dogs were. He let them all loose again to quickly get them out of danger."

Out of twenty sled dogs, four were missing. Grout went out five times looking for the dogs. At one point over the next three weeks, thirty people searched for the dogs by snowmobile and from the air. They even placed legs of lamb in strategic areas to lure them back, but to no avail. Dog tracks were seen twenty-five miles away within a crevasse field, leading some to surmise that the dogs may have fallen to their deaths. The setback drew heat from animal rights activists when it was apparent the missing dogs more likely perished from starvation.

Norman would later write to an online community of some 300,000 who were following the expedition on Prodigy, "This was an awful experience. But a setback like this only strengthens the persistency to continue."

Not one to waste any time, Norman and his team tried again in January 1994, but were grounded for sixteen days by weather. Time had run out, and the second attempt was scrubbed. The cancellation was another major blow; undaunted, the team traveled a few weeks later to New York to raise funds for yet another try in late 1994.

At the time, Norman was wearing Vent-a-Layer expedition clothing from my client, Duofold, and we spoke about the plane crash and dog tragedy often, once over a memorable dinner under the vaulted tile ceiling of the famed Oyster Bar in New York's Grand Central Station. There I was, a "suit" in his forties, with this famed explorer right out of the pages of *National Geographic*—snow white beard, Andy Rooney eyebrows, dozens of lines and scars across his face, each with a story to tell. I remember fondly Norman challenging me to a garlic-eating contest. I lost. The main lesson learned was never get into a competition with someone who probably grew up consuming seal meat and beef jerky or whatever else Byrd was feeding his men.

He called me "Mister Big-Time PR Super Operator." Coming from this white-haired adventurer who looked like he stepped out of a diorama in the American Museum of Natural History, I took it as a high compliment.

Thus, as a Super Operator, how could I resist when the opportunity came to organize his press conference at The Explorers Club?

The resulting press coverage included a one-third-page story in the *New York Post*, packed with puns and silly word play. HE'S HOT TO CONQUER ANTARCTICA—AT 88 read the headline. In a stroke of good timing, it was snowing during the press conference, so the photographer had Norman pose outside throwing a snowball. The caption read, SNOWBALLING AMBITIONS: NORMAN VAUGHAN'S DREAMS HAVEN'T GONE TO MUSH.

Norman resumed the attempt in early December 1994, this time without sled dogs because of a new Antarctic treaty that banned them. The seven-member expedition included Norman's fourth wife, Carolyn Muegge-Vaughan, thirty-seven years his junior; Vern Tejas (a "Seven Summiteer" who climbed the tallest peaks on each continent); Gordon Wiltsie, climber and guide for Adventure Network International; and a *National Geographic* television film crew.

The evening before the final ascent of Mount Vaughan, Vern and the Vaughans camped out in a crevasse 900 feet below the summit. Norman wore dark sunglasses both outside and inside his tent to counteract a mild case of snow blindness.

In an interview, Vern told the Associated Press what frustrated Norman the most: "He has the mind of a student and the heart of a child, but the body of an older person, and that slows him down."

Gordon remembered years later, "A young, fit climber probably could have ascended Mount Vaughan in a few hours. Ultimately (and partly due to weather) it would take Norman nine days, but I was still astonished by his fortitude."

According to Elizabeth Royte, writing for *LIFE Magazine,* Vern and Gordon chopped and stamped 7,000 steps into the snow- and ice-covered mountain to help Norman summit his namesake peak, hampered by a plastic and metal right knee and a fused right ankle. After this successful first-ever ascent on December 16, 1994, just three days shy of his eighty-ninth birthday, Norman read an emotional message: ". . . By climbing this mountain for my eighty-ninth birthday, I dared to fail. . . . Dream big, dream big young and old, and dare to fail. I have fulfilled a sixty-five-year-old dream.

"This climb is also in tribute to the tenacious spirit of the Antarctic sled dogs who never gave up. They have been my inspiration."

Afterward, Carolyn attempted to light eighty-nine sparklers on the snowy summit of "Norman's Giant Birthday Cake," but the wind was too strong to ignite them. The team then remained overnight, beginning their twelve-hour descent the next morning after planting an Explorers Club flag and taking plenty of photos for sponsors.

In later years, when money was tight, Colonel Vaughan often worked as a consultant to corporations involved in the outdoors. He posed in the *New York Times Fashion of the Times* magazine wearing a $650 Ralph Lauren hand-knit cable-stitched turtleneck in a photo spread that included astronaut Buzz Aldrin.

One year he also lent his name to a Timberland-sponsored "Trip of a Lifetime" sweepstakes. Twenty-four lucky consumers and store personnel were invited to four of Latin America's most challenging destinations. One of the three freelance "Timberland Athletes" leading the group was Vaughan, then ninety. Perhaps it wasn't the most prestigious thing to do after being Admiral Byrd's chief dog musher, but Norman needed to raise awareness, and at least Timberland had a strong connection with outdoor adventure.

During the Timberland trip, he passed the time regaling fellow travelers with anecdotes about Admiral Byrd. He told of Byrd instructing his team to wear the same underwear for ten days, then switch to new pairs, then after twenty days go back to the old pairs. In a twisted sense of polar logic, that's how team members convinced themselves they had clean underwear.

"Boy, they felt good," Norman chuckled.

Inducted into the Musher Hall of Fame in 1990, he organized and led the 776-mile Norman Vaughan's Serum Run, an annual dogsled and snowmobile competition that commemorates the twenty men and their dog teams who relayed crucial diphtheria serum from Alaska's Nenana to Nome in 1925. During that fateful year, a potentially fatal diphtheria outbreak in Nome required emergency delivery of serum to stricken residents. Weather conditions prevented shipment by air, so twenty dog teams were assembled to convey the much-needed medicine over land.

Norman accurately predicted that he would live to be 100 years of age, "because not many people die after that," he joked with *Lonely Planet* guidebook author Jeff Rubin. For years he had plans to return to the summit of Mount Vaughan to celebrate his 100th birthday, perhaps with a sip of champagne, which would be the first taste of alcohol for this lifelong teetotaler.

A lack of funds dashed that hope to return to Mount Vaughan, but, ever the optimist, Norman had a back-up plan: a birthday party in a mountainside restaurant in Telluride, Colorado. I was representing the Hotel Telluride at the time and was all over this, distributing press material to national media.

Norman was originally set to fly to the hotel for the celebration, but ill health just one week prior kept him grounded in his hometown of Anchorage. He died just four days after his 100th birthday on December 23, 2005.

In *My Life of Adventure* (Stackpole Books, 1995), Norman sums up his philosophy of life with a simple, yet inspiring catchphrase: "Dream Big and Dare to Fail." And if you don't like that motto, he had another he would lay on you faster than a sled dog: "The only death you die is the death you die everyday by not living."

Today Carolyn Muegge-Vaughan says that he remains an inspiration to countless people who tell her how their lives were touched and even dramatically changed by Norman.

His was not the most scientific of expeditions. In fact, it was utterly brilliant in its simplicity. Just one man, one mountain, and a nation of armchair explorers following along.

Climbing for Dollars

Tying in with a nonprofit—preferably a compelling cause that can attract sponsors and media attention—can be a successful technique to partially fund your adventure or expedition. According to Freddie Wilkinson, writing in the March 2009 *Rock and Ice* magazine, "In the last two decades, charity climbing has grown into a cottage industry complete with specialty guides, motivational speakers, and fund-raising consultants—the vast majority of which focus on the Seven Summits (the tallest peaks on each continent) and a handful of other well-known peaks like Mount Rainier or the Eiger."

How do you select the most appropriate cause to support? You're not going to find it in a book. It has to come from the heart. Or your own personal experience.

"Everyone knows someone who has been stricken with cancer, so think about creating a fund-raiser for cancer research or one of a thousand other worthy causes," advises Rick Wilcox, an experienced search-and-rescue volunteer in New Hampshire's White Mountains. Rick has led fifty expeditions above 18,000 feet, some twenty-five in the Himalayas alone, and currently owns International Mountain Equipment, an outdoor store and climbing school in North Conway. One year I hired Rick and his staff to lead a group of media up the steep and rocky four-mile trail from the Appalachian Mountain Club lodge in Pinkham Notch to Tuckerman Ravine, site of famed late-season gonzo skiing and snowboarding on Mount Washington.

Rick gets a pained look on his face when asked about how his clientele attempt to secure sponsors for outdoor projects: "I tell them, 'don't come to me looking for sponsorship.' Not a week goes by that someone doesn't want me to donate a spot on one of my trips. I tell them I'm a 'try for profit' company and that they need to seek funding elsewhere, but certainly not from any of my guides. They live in their cars. You need to find a sponsor with money."

Laura Evans' cause was breast cancer, a disease she knew only too well. In 1990, Laura was at the end of her seventh week in isolation during a bone marrow transplant. She was fighting stage-three breast cancer when she hit upon an idea: form a team of breast cancer survivors to climb a mountain to raise awareness and financial support to fight the disease.

She pitched the idea to renowned mountain guide Peter Whittaker, son of mountaineering legend Lou Whittaker, who led her on an unsuccessful attempt to summit Washington State's Mount Rainier in 1983.

"I want to climb a bigger mountain, I'm ready for a bigger mountain, and I want to do it for breast cancer, with other survivors. It would send an incredible message about survival, will and hope," she writes in *The Climb of My Life* (HarperSanFrancisco, 1996). Peter would christen the project "Expedition Inspiration."

JanSport, maker of packs, tents, and apparel, was the first sponsor to recognize this potential to generate positive publicity while it assisted a worthy cause. Other outdoor companies, including Duofold, LEKI, Marmot, Moving Comfort, Outdoor Research, Raichle, and Salomon, soon followed. Outdoor magazines got into the spirit with donations of free ad space and glowing news coverage; Laura and Peter were even featured on the cover of the industry trade publication, *Sporting Goods Business*.

In February 1995, the two led a team of sixteen breast-cancer survivors to Argentina's Mount Aconcagua, which at 22,841 feet is the highest mountain in the world outside of the Himalayas. She writes about that day on the summit, "Twelve days, eleven hours, and forty minutes after we had physically begun this journey, we were truly on top of the world. We were euphoric that we had made it, grinning ear-to-ear as we took that last step onto the narrow platform that formed the summit. Three breast-cancer survivors standing proudly, arm in arm, happy to be alive, more alive than ever at 23,000 feet."

Laura died in 2000 at the age of fifty-one in her home in Ketchum, Idaho, but the Expedition Inspiration Fund for Breast Cancer Research continues. Since then, the organization has arranged several successful expeditions, various "Take-a-Hike" events, symposia, and other fundraising activities across the United States. Thousands of women and men are inspired by the efforts of Expedition Inspiration, which all started with Laura's effort to combine her love of the outdoors with a desire to help others. She writes, "In order to survive, it takes one small courageous uphill step at a time" (expeditioninspiration.org).

In April 2001, Robert Chang, an experienced mountaineer and guide from Santa Clara, California, lost his sister, Marie, to a rare form of cancer. By that fall he and friends successfully climbed Island Peak, a 20,305-foot mountain in the Nepal Himalayas, in her memory. His "Climbing for a Cure" project is dedicated to climbing high peaks throughout the world's greatest mountain ranges to promote the prevention, education, and support activities of its cancer-project partners. Companies from The North Face to AlpineAire to MSR and Nalgene lined up to sponsor the effort. We helped him receive support from Wacoal Sports Science Corporation, makers of CW-X Conditioning Wear. He returned the favor by posing at 24,000-foot Camp III on Mount Everest for a humorous video testimonial dubbed the "world's highest altitude fashion show." It was great fun, all for a terrific cause (climbingforacure.com).

The Fred Hutchinson Cancer Research Center in Seattle organized an Alaskan climb in 2008 to raise awareness for cancer research. The Big Expedition for Cancer Research targeted a previously unclimbed mountain with the help of a Mountaineering Advisory Committee—a climbing Dream Team if there ever was one: Phil and Susan Ershler, the first couple to climb the world's fabled Seven Summits; John Harlin, a noted climber and editor of *American Alpine Journal*; Eric Simonson, leader of the historic Mount Everest expedition that found the body of George Leigh Mallory; John Roskelley, a public servant, conservationist, author, and revered American Himalayan climber; and Jim Wickwire, the first American to climb K2, the second-highest mountain on earth.

On June 21, 2008, the team of four mountaineers determined that they had reached the safe limits of their attempt. For nine hours, they battled unstable snow, ice, and rock to move within 500 vertical feet of the summit of Peak 8290 in Glacier Bay's Fairweather Range. The conditions prevented them from safely climbing higher. The two rope teams huddled at the high point and called an end to the expedition.

"Extremely hazardous" were the first two words out of Seattle climber Matt Farmer's mouth when he made the satellite phone call back from base camp. "We gave this mountain everything we had within the bound-

aries of safe, rational mountaineering standards. Sometimes the mountain sets the limits and we have to accept them," Farmer said.

While they may not have successfully summited, thousands of people
followed the climb in the media and online, thus helping to raise awareness of the critical need for cancer research (fhcrc.org).

Another example of dedicating an adventure or expedition to raising funds and awareness is the Sagarmatha Environmental Expedition of
1994, which decided not just to climb Everest, but to remove at least one
ton of garbage from the mountain's high camps. Sherpas were paid an in-
centive of $2 to $6 per load, beyond their salaries, to ferry used paper and
plastics, batteries, oxygen bottles, and other detritus from years of climbs,
an era when the mountain was treated as a trash pit. "It was a pragmatic
approach to solve a problem," said American team member Scott Fischer,
who would later tragically die on the mountain in 1996. "The Sherpas are
paid to go up; why not pay them to bring trash down?" Many sponsors
apparently agreed. The expedition succeeded in receiving support from
High Sierra, Sierra Sport, and 3M Thinsulate Thermal Insulation, among
other companies.

Some organizations plan guided expeditions you can join in exchange
for a fund-raising commitment. Once accepted into the program, you're
expected to approach friends, family, and local businesses for their tax-
deductible support. For instance, the American Foundation for Children
with AIDS (AFCA) offers fund-raising treks to Africa's Mount Kilimanjaro to raise money to provide medication and medical supplies for
children with HIV/AIDS in sub-Saharan Africa. Teams consist of twelve
climbers, each of whom commits to raising funds for AFCA.

Tanya Weaver, AFCA's executive director, says, "We think the challenge of climbing to the summit of Mount Kilimanjaro is an appropriate symbol for the uphill battle HIV/AIDS children face" (helpchildrenwithAIDS.org, climbupsokidscangrowup.com).

Answer the "So What" Question

☞ **Study Those Who Came Before**—Become a student of adventurers and explorers. Read books, view documentaries, and learn from others' past mistakes. If you want to tour the Amazon, become an authority on the region. When the British explorer Robert Swan was soliciting funds for his 1985–86 "In the Footsteps of Scott Expedition," which traced the route of the ill-fated Capt. Robert Falcon Scott expedition, he pitched corporations that had previously sponsored Scott.

"After studying Scott's archives and letters, Swan met with Shell Oil. 'You supported Scott back then,' he told them, 'why not support me in 1985?' Shell pledged $220,000 in gasoline and lubricating oil. A similar ploy worked with Burberry, which supplied Scott's clothing," writes Mike Cannell in the *New York Times*.

Swan would later famously say of his expedition that it was " . . . the cleanest and most isolated way of having a bad time ever devised. . . . But it pumps up your ego."

☞ **Develop a Compelling Hook**—Studying previous expeditions will provide insight into how your project will be different in one way or another. Without a strong hook, there's little chance your project will attract media attention. No media attention means a lackluster response from prospective sponsors. Assuming you're not planning to pay for it all yourself, you'll need to attract sponsors with a project that somehow makes a difference in how we understand the environment, the geography of a region, the human condition, or the limits of human performance. Pick a project that will also resonate in the media.

☞ **Instill Confidence**—A potential sponsor is about to stake his hard-earned reputation on your project. Instill a sense of confidence. Explain how every project you've undertaken in the past leads to this one. Anticipate a sponsor's objections and detail how you plan to accomplish your goal safely and with a high degree of integrity. In other words, do your homework.

☞ **Seek a Charitable Tie-in**—There are hundreds, if not thousands of worthy nonprofit organizations that are in desperate need of support. By selecting one that's near and dear to your heart, your project will stand for something bigger than your own individual goals. Not only will you be supporting a worthy cause, but your project will become more attractive to corporate sponsors and more palatable to media considering coverage.

Do Your Homework

People often ask me how many expeditions I've been on. Sadly, not many. Sometimes it seems as if you have to be dirt poor to be able to join an expedition and not have any financial obligations pulling you back home. Or else you're among the wealthy who can delegate underlings to take the helm while you trek around the world.

For the rest of us in the middle—those, say, who have to work for a living—that adventure or expedition project needs to be carefully planned to coincide with vacation time, holidays, or perhaps a sabbatical or leave of absence.

When the time does come to seek sponsorship, corporations or private individuals supporting you want to be assured that they're not sending you off to your death. They want to know that you've invested personal time and money to become experienced, you know your way around an ice axe and can self-arrest, you have at least modest communications skills, and you have the leadership capabilities to bring a team together to achieve a common goal. In other words, do you have the right stuff to pull this off?

Often it helps to gain experience by becoming a member of someone else's team—someone more knowledgeable about what can go wrong, how to communicate the project to the media, and the importance of networking with other adventurers and explorers.

"Men wanted for hazardous journey, small wages, bitter cold, long months of complete darkness, constant danger, safe return doubtful, honor and recognition in case of success."

        —Ernest Shackleton advertisement reportedly placed in 1913

Welcome Aboard: Join Someone Else's Expedition First

If you're just starting out, and you're relatively unknown but have aspirations to be the next great adventurer or explorer, hitch your wagon to a star. That's exactly what Icelander Gunnar Marel Eggertsson achieved when he set his sights on commemorating what is arguably the greatest expedition of all time—the discovery of the New World.

When you call a potential sponsor out of the blue with a seemingly foolhardy scheme to sail a replica Viking ship from Iceland to Newfoundland (home of the only authenticated Viking site in North America), then to continue sailing to St. John's, Halifax, Boston, Providence, Mystic Seaport, New Haven, and New York, you'll have to excuse the silence on the other end of the line. But Gunnar was determined to prove he had the goods—the experience, the determination, and the drive—to recreate the most famous voyage of Leif Eriksson, the most celebrated Icelander of all time, of whom he was a direct descendant.

Millions grew up singing the Christopher Columbus song, *In fourteen hundred ninety-two Columbus sailed the ocean blue. . . .*

Of that there's no denying. But Gunnar, the grandson of a celebrated Icelandic shipbuilder and captain, had a problem—a serious problem— with the renowned Columbus and his claim to be first to discover the New World. Gunnar was convinced that Vikings from his native Iceland first stumbled across the North American continent in the year 1000.

Gunnar wasn't the only passenger on the bash-Columbus train. The Iceland Tourist Board, by then a long-time client of mine, saw in Gunnar's dream a publicity gold mine. Iceland President Olafur Ragnar Grimsson told me at the time, "If Americans want to celebrate Columbus' discovery of 1492, they can go right ahead. But to us, he was a latecomer."

Gunnar realized that he couldn't rest on the laurels of his famous ancestor. To raise the kind of money he sought, he had to demonstrate that he knew port from starboard, that he had the right chops. He was born in 1954 into a family of shipbuilders on the Westman Islands, small islands off the southern shore of Iceland best known as the scene of a horrific volcanic eruption in 1973 that destroyed 417 properties in sixty-plus feet of lava and ash. By the age of twenty-five, he was a fully educated shipbuilder who dreamed of making a name for himself.

In 1990, a small accident that broke his arm grounded him for four months. While recovering, he came across a Norwegian plan to sail a Viking ship replica called *Gaia* from Norway to Washington, D.C. He knew he had to be part of that adventure.

Gunnar wrote a simple five-line request for employment to leaders of the Gaia Expedition, which hoped to arrive in America in 1991, to preempt celebrations the following year commemorating the 500th anniversary of Columbus' arrival in the New World. Gunnar emphasized his experience as a diver, captain, and shipbuilder and was soon accepted into the crew as second in command. He set sail in May 1991 from the replica's homeport on the west coast of Norway. Ahead of them lay the cold, iceberg-infested waters of Iceland, Greenland, Labrador, and Newfoundland. From there, the ship sailed as far south as Washington, D.C., arriving in October of that year.

Later he participated in another Gaia voyage from Washington, D.C., to Rio de Janeiro, arriving in time to help open a UN environmental conference, all the while dreaming of his own expedition.

In 1994, he decided to literally build a Viking ship with his own hands. But even with solid experience under his belt, he found the sponsorship fund-raising effort tough going. "It was a battle for me," he remembered during our meeting in 2008 at Iceland's famed Blue Lagoon spa. "I was so convinced of the importance of commemorating Leif Eriksson's voyage that they would have had to shoot me to stop me from doing this," Gunnar explained in heavily accented English punctuated at the end of many sentences by a quick gasp of air—sort of a sharp inhale—that's a peculiarity of many of my Icelandic friends.

Finally, with the help of the Icelandic ambassador to the U.S., he raised the necessary funds to construct a replica Viking ship called the *Islendingur* ("Icelander"). It was a seventy-five-foot wooden Viking longboat, the kind used during the settlement of the country from 870 to 930 AD and an almost exact duplicate of the *Gokstad*, an 870 AD ship unearthed in 1882 on a farm in southern Norway. Thanks to a burial in soil rich in blue clay, the ship's wood was almost perfectly preserved and is currently on display at the Viking Ship Museum in Oslo.

With the aid of a shipbuilding friend, Gunnar carefully selected the *Islendingur's* wood—pine and oak from Norway and Sweden. The sail was sewn in Denmark, on the advice of Norwegian Jon Godal, a world authority on Viking ships.

Gunnar's plan was to trace the historic 2,600-mile voyage of Leif "The Lucky" Eriksson to Greenland and Newfoundland—the country the Vikings called Vinland—exactly 1,000 years earlier. Leif's father, Erik the Red, was one of the great polar scam artists of all times. Banished from Iceland for three years, he sailed westward to look for a land that had been sighted some sixty years earlier. "Green Land," he would call it, a land of even greater opportunity than his homeland with the frigid name. He said, "People will be attracted thither, if the land has a good name," according to the early sagas.

Gunnar, who determined through genealogical research that he's a straight-line descendant of Leif's grandfather, spent one year building the *Islendingur* with methods and tools based as closely as possible on those used by the original Vikings. He built it as authentically as possible, right down to the Viking-style bathroom (literally a bucket in a small closet), a steer board in the stern, a dragonhead at the bow, and Viking shields flanking the port and starboard rails. One of his few concessions to modernity was a self-inflating life raft on deck, which he kept cleverly hidden under a sheepskin blanket, a marine VHF radio, and an engine to help the ship dock in busy ports, the theory being that it would be hard to recruit sixty-four rowers to power the ship the true Viking way.

Starting on June 17, 2000, Iceland Independence Day, Gunnar, then age forty-five, sailed to North America with a crew of seven men and one woman.

The 4,000-mile, four-month journey gave them all an appreciation for how lucky Leif must have been. The crew fought for their lives for ten hours off the southern tip of Greenland, battling dangerous pack ice on a foggy, stormy night that July. The rest of the time, they had to contend with mosquitoes that attacked the crew's hands and faces, pods of whales that threatened to collide with the ship, and visibility of as little as seventy-five feet in the midst of ice fields.

Ellen Ingvadottir, the lone woman in the crew, described what it was like creeping along in fog. According to her Web site diary, "Traveling in an open ship in thick fog creates a strange feeling of calm. Yet [there is] some concern as to what lies ahead. Modern technology and good navigation charts make the journey easier today, whereas voyaging in such conditions a thousand years ago was quite different. Certainly, the fog and the cold mist settling on your skin were the same, but everything else was different."

Earlier she wrote, "Standing rudder duty at nightfall when the fog sets in is quite an experience. Your mind begins to wander as you glance regularly at the compass and then up front and around the ship, trying to see through the fog whether there are any obstacles in the Viking ship's path, including hazardous icebergs coming from the north."

Over 1,000 years ago, the sight of a Viking ship in your harbor was about as welcome as a hurricane, given the propensity of Vikings to rape, pillage, and generally carry on as world-class plunderers. But in 2000, the ship was welcomed to Newfoundland's northernmost tip by 15,000 people who came to relive history. The arrival was broadcast live throughout Canada. Hotels, motels, and bed and breakfasts were all jammed to capacity as people came to see the ship and listen to music, enjoy local choir performances, buy souvenirs from street vendors, and partake in a Millennium feast.

In the town of Norris Point, Newfoundland (population 786), over 2,000 visited the ship in four hours on a single day; in nearby Harbour Breton, and then again in Burin on the south coast of the province, vessels sounded ten-minute greetings on their horns. The *Islendingur* was met with equal fanfare at stops further down the coast.

For its long-awaited arrival in New York Harbor on October 5, 2000, the ship's twenty-sixth port of call since the previous June, my staff was ready with their press kits, media lists, cell phones, and cameras. This was New York, the media capital of the world; we could leave nothing to chance. Our clients, the Iceland Tourist Board and a cooperative marketing association called IcelandNaturally, wanted to make a big splash, so we arranged a media reception in New York at the South Street Seaport on the East River. But first we had to sail the boat there.

Knowing full-well my propensity for seasickness—*mal de mer*, tossing your cookies, praying to the porcelain god, call it what you like—under certain conditions I could be incapacitated, or at the very least, the front of my shirt severely stained. As the saying goes, once afflicted you become afraid you're going to die; then as seasickness gets worse, you worry that you won't. I wear seasickness as a badge of honor. After all, no less an explorer than Charles Darwin was famously prone to the condition, resting in a hammock and eating only raisins during rough passages, and spending as much time ashore as possible.

Some people work for money, others for the experiences work can bring to make a fuller life. I do it for both. That's what has made mine an extraordinary career. Certainly, not once in a twenty-five-year career has it ever been boring. Thus, if there's an opportunity to do something different, travel somewhere I haven't been, I'll jump at the chance, despite the possibility that I might wind up curled in a fetal position on the deck of a fake Viking ship holding my stomach and whimpering like a two-year-old. I was willing to risk such embarrassment when I decided to jump aboard the *Islendingur* at the American Yacht Club in Rye, New York, for the boat's final leg into New York Harbor.

Thanks to ceaseless pitch calls and emails to TV and radio assignment desks, and newspaper and magazine editors, I managed to convince a reporter named Morrie Alter from WCBS-TV to join us. Morrie was a master at telling stories in three minutes, the kind of news stories that go beyond the random fire or murder. Stories with heart, stories you'll long remember. "Little movies," he would call them.

So there was Morrie waiting to board the ship at the Yacht Club, with videographer in tow. I was there, slightly zoned out on Dramamine, but otherwise ready to roll. As we entered New York Harbor, the CBS 2 News traffic helicopter hovered overhead. Morrie conducted his live stand-up looking straight up into the copter's swivel-mounted camera, as the station cut live to its coverage of the ship's arrival.

Meanwhile, Ruth Burton, a freelance event specialist working with us, was waiting at the South Street Seaport, having arranged a location for the media to welcome the ship. Recalling how Gunnar's organizers successfully secured a fireboat welcome in Boston, it was her job to contact the New York City Fire Department for a similar wet welcome in Manhattan.

I remember asking Ruth for an update on her discussion with the FDNY.

"They want to know what colors you want them to dye the water," she said.

"They can do colors?" I asked in amazement.

Who knew? We ordered five gallons of blue and five gallons of red dye, two of the colors of Iceland, for about $390 and had a photo opportunity that publicists kill for.

The New York media reception was followed over the next few days by a public viewing of the Viking ship, complete with historical displays, Icelandic musical entertainment, and samples of Icelandic foods, including dried fish and smoked lamb, and a particularly nasty dish called hakarl—dried, petrified shark with a vile, putrid smell.

The sponsors even had someone dressed up in a puffin suit to prance around Pier 17 to interact with kids. I was a bit uneasy about the puffin mascot since just a few steps away, adults were scarfing samples of broiled puffins, an Icelandic delicacy, being passed out on food trays. Personally, I have a rule never to eat a country's signature bird. That goes for American bald eagles as well as the favorite bird of my client's homeland.

A few weeks later we would organize a Hudson River reception on the Viking ship at the 79th Street Boat Basin. Iceland president Olafur Ragnar Grimsson was there along with the country's First Lady, Dorrit Moussaieff, a jewelry designer, editor, and socialite who through her society connections hosted the singer Diana Ross and industrialist George Soros at the party. Since a traditional Viking bathroom was deemed somewhat unsuitable for the bold-face names attending the party, we rented a tired liveaboard yacht at the marina, the seventy-three-foot *Argo*, just to use its head. Folks say, "Don't sweat the small stuff." Well, in the event-planning business, it's all small stuff. We anticipated that with a bunch of party-going Icelanders aboard the Viking ship, drinking the country's nasty schnapps concoction called Brennivin, we would need at least one bathroom a bit more upscale than a pail in a closet.

Gunnar's arrival in New York was a public relations home run. Besides the live coverage on WCBS, there were more live shots on the *CBS Early Show*, *Fox News*, WABC-TV, and WNBC-TV, plus a half-page story in the *New York Times*.

Times reporter Jon Tierney took a decidedly local slant to the Viking ship's arrival by postulating that Vikings once roamed Brooklyn, specifically Gowanus Bay. In a half-page story, he quotes Gunnar as supporting this thesis: "'The Vikings had really seaworthy ships and were very curious,' the Icelandic captain said. 'They wanted to find new land, and they could easily sail down the coast. It would have taken them only a month or two from their base in Canada. It's clear to me from reading the sagas that they got at least as far as New York.'"

Tierney, who traveled with us into New York Harbor, showed Gunnar modern-day photos of Gowanus Bay, including the infamous and particularly odorous Gowanus Canal. Could Gunnar's ancestors have actually wintered along these shores? "Yes," Gunnar is resolutely quoted in the *Times* story, "the Vikings could have stopped there. It was nicer at the time."

Gunnar's main sponsor, the Leif Eriksson Millennium Commission of Iceland, retained an independent media monitoring service that tracked over thirty newspaper stories, representing a total circulation of 25.4 million. Then, by adding up the column inches of exposure and calculating it against the cost to advertise in those papers, they estimated that the publicity had an equivalent ad value of $5.6 million. The TV exposure had a more modest $635,000 in ad equivalency.

Now here's where it becomes interesting: Since the *Islendingur* exposure was generated in the form of newspaper and TV stories, and people buy newspapers and watch TV for the news, not the ads and commercials, ad equivalency is only part of the story. What about believability? Media coverage is a lot more believable than advertising (apologies to those of you who work on Madison Avenue). Thus, if it's more believable, it's worth more than advertising. Public relations executives agree it's at least three times more believable. Thus, by that measurement, the *Islendingur* generated the total ad equivalency multiplied by three—a whopping $18.7 million in marketing value. Any way you look at it, for the two Icelandic sponsors, the project represented great return on their investment.

You'd think that with results like that, Gunnar would have had sponsors lining up at his cabin door for phase two of the voyage. Unfortunately for him, that was not the case.

For a time, the ship languished in Brewer Pilot Points Marina in Westbrook, Connecticut, as Gunnar sought a buyer.

Fast forward almost a full year to late summer 2001 when Gunnar had finally scraped together enough support from Swedish telecom operator Telia to leave Westbrook and continue his East Coast tour. This time the ship was headed to Washington, D.C., where it would arrive in time to promote the launch of Telia's new Viking Network.

The contract for $190,000 in sponsorship support was being finalized when the 9/11 attacks occurred. In fact, the executive at Telia, to whom Gunnar had pitched so diligently to pony up sponsorship funding, watched from his Washington-area office as American Airlines Flight 77 hit the Pentagon. Plans for future use of the Viking replica ship immediately sank.

Afterward, Eggertsson had hoped to sell *Islendingur* to a museum, or to the government of Iceland, but, alas, there was not much demand for a slightly used Viking ship by then, especially one without a bathroom. At one time, the ship, still in dry-dock in Connecticut, was listed on eBaymotors.com for $618,500. It received just one bid, which failed to meet the reserve.

Gunnar flew home deep in debt, leaving behind the *Islendingur* to collect dust in dry-dock.

"I had to behave like a lunatic to raise money," he said. Eventually, he sold a 90 percent share in the boat, and it was returned to Iceland via container ship.

Now the *Islendingur* sits on supports along a nondescript stretch of highway leading into Reykjavik. It is destined to become the centerpiece for the permanent home of *Vikings: The North Atlantic Saga*, the Smithsonian Institution exhibition that previously toured the U.S.

The ship will become a new tourist attraction, Gunnar hopes, although local Icelandic officials are calling the display "Viking World," a name he intensely dislikes because of its similarity to Disney World.

"It's a bad name. It won't be nearly as large."

Gunnar has reverted back to his carpentry skills. He is one adventurer who fifteen years ago dreamed of the trip of a lifetime and eventually, through the sheer force of his willpower and determination, and a stint as an apprentice on someone else's expedition, found the financial support he needed to honor his adventurous forefather.

Plan a Trial Run

No self-respecting pilot would take off in a new plane that wasn't first test flown. Think sponsors enjoy a warm and fuzzy feeling about funding an Everest expedition if the climber has never been on a big mountain before? The same goes for a businessman planning to muscle a bizarre pedal-powered boat across the Atlantic.

Dwight Collins completed his homework and planned a trial run so well that it led to a change in the very nature of his expedition.

A Noroton, Connecticut, real estate developer, Dwight wanted one final adventure in the early 1990s before marriage, one final physical challenge before the obligations of family and business would forever lock him into the stable, if not the stifling confines of a nine-to-five job in the family business.

Dwight, then thirty-three, was an avid sea kayaker, University of Pennsylvania graduate cum laude, and a former U.S. Navy SEAL who knew a renowned marine architect in nearby Rowayton, a small river town on the southern shore of Connecticut. Bruce Kirby was best known for designing the Laser, *Canada I* (an America's Cup yacht), the one-design Sonar and more recently, the Pixel sailboat. Dwight approached him to design a twenty-three-foot pedal-powered boat using a bicycle hub and foot pedals that would allow him to literally "bike" his way across the pond. In fact, the project was dubbed "Biking the Atlantic," in a nod to adventurer Ned Gillette who believed project titles should be as self-descriptive as possible. Years earlier, Ned's own adventure was dubbed "Row the Atlantic," which, well, is exactly what he accomplished as I'll explain later.

What drove Dwight to attempt this feat? He would later tell *Sports Illustrated,* "In life everything is gray, but the idea of pedaling the Atlantic was clear, simple, straightforward, and it had never been done." Dwight was inspired by his reading of *A Fighting Chance: How We Rowed Across the Atlantic in 92 Days* (J. B. Lippincott, 1966) by Scottish yachtsman Chay Blyth who, in 1966, rowed with Captain John Ridgway across the Atlantic in ninety-two days in an open twenty-foot dory. After reading

Blyth's account, Dwight spent over twenty years compiling data about trans-Atlantic crossings and human-powered vehicles.

But would this be a solo effort or could he find a kindred spirit, someone with the same drive and passion for adventure? He found that person in Robert Wells, a then forty-seven-year-old New York advertising executive who in July 1991 raced his road bike from the Canadian border 350 miles to the Long Island Sound in less than twenty hours—his wife, Barbara, dutifully following behind in the family car. Still, Wells considered himself a "plain brown wrapper" kind of guy who wanted to demonstrate how anything is possible if you put your mind to it.

About that time, I became aware of the project and agreed to help promote and raise funds for the effort, scheduled for the summer of 1992. A pedal-powered crossing of the Atlantic in an odd-looking craft was no crazier than a dogsled trek to the North Pole or the first nonmechanized crossing of Antarctica. Besides, who was I—a publicist who spends days chained to a keyboard—to judge the epic from the foolhardy, the record-breaking from the suicidal? Sure, I knew a thing or two about sea kayaking from my days working for the North American Paddlesports Association, and I was getting pretty good at promoting expeditions, but this project was a bit worrisome.

Sponsors, I knew, become a bit squirrelly about funding expeditions that could prove fatal to the inexperienced adventurer. Sponsoring golf or tennis tournaments? That they understand. But an attempt at the fastest human-powered crossing of the Atlantic would be a bit difficult to justify to the board of directors. Even if the craft is watertight, fully enclosed, and self-righting. Even if the adventurer is a competitive swimmer who once swam 28.5 miles around Manhattan in eight hours fifty-four minutes and harbored no obvious signs of a death wish.

Sponsorship was critical. With $30,000 of his own money sunk in the project, Dwight was short about $120,000—a common affliction among adventurers and explorers. Just because you want to pedal across the Atlantic doesn't mean corporate America needs to line up to fund your dream. I agreed to take on the marketing challenge before me: convincing corporate America that the two adventurers had the right stuff to spend upwards of forty days battling the Atlantic together.

Bob and Dwight developed a sponsorship package that offered the stars and the moon. Climb aboard as a title sponsor, and your company name and logo would appear on the hull. It would be called the Your Name Here Trans-Atlantic Crossing. Sponsors could entertain clients at the beginning and end, use the boat in their advertising, appear in a documentary, and sample their products during a promotional tour.

But apparently it wasn't enough. "I knew dozens of companies through the ad agency where I worked," Bob told me years later. "ATT, GE, IBM, XEROX, I had contacts at all of them but it was a big dry hole. I couldn't convince any of them that two human beings doing something extraordinary would be a great project that could inspire their employees."

We all felt that to attract sponsors, the project needed visibility well before their actual Atlantic crossing began.

On a summer day in 1991, Dwight met me on the Connecticut coast, not far from his home. There in dry-dock was this bright orange-and-white human-powered boat, one unlike any I had ever seen.

I asked Dwight rather indelicately, "What's the furthest you've pedaled in that thing?"

"We've been all over the Western Connecticut coastline," he replied.

I was underwhelmed. I knew he had also logged some 4,000 hours on a recumbent bicycle in his living room, but what the project needed was more water time in the 850-pound self-righting carbon fiber and cedar craft he called *Tango* after his first wedding dance with his wife Corinne.

It was then that we hatched a plan to have Bob and Dwight spend some quality time together pedaling from New York's South Street Seaport to Boston Harbor, a distance of approximately 300 miles, including a particularly difficult passage through the Cape Cod Canal into Cape Cod Bay. The trial run, we reasoned, could gain more publicity exposure, which could lead to more sponsors, and test various assumptions about the meal plan and durability of the mechanical equipment on board.

After many calls and meetings, Bob found a friend at Schieffelin & Somerset who agreed to provide $35,000 in seed money to support the trial run on behalf of Moët & Chandon champagne. Aura Reinhardt, the company's vice president of public relations in charge of Moët, was particularly enthusiastic, reasoning that champagne has long been a part of ocean-going crossings. Champagne is a part of christening ceremonies: "It's the beverage of celebration," she gushed to Shari Caudron writing in *Industry Week*.

Champagne is quaffed by the gallons during ocean crossings (think Noel Coward sloshing across the Atlantic on the *Queen Mary*). And to celebrate a sailboat race, as much champagne is spilled as it is consumed. So there was indeed logic in securing a bubbly sponsor.

Biking the Atlantic was still grossly underfunded, despite the influx of cash from Schieffelin & Somerset. But what it lacked in cash, it made up for with a veritable Sports Authority worth of in-kind sponsors. Cascade Designs provided dry bags, Sony equipped the team with an early version GPS unit called the PYXIS, Malden Mills gave them Polartec clothing, and the bottom of the craft was painted with Sea-Slide, a coating that can improve drag reduction by 10 percent. For emergencies, they carried a Medical Sea Pak, which was so complete they could have delivered a baby.

The food plan included AlpineAire freeze-dried foods, Exceed high-carbohydrate sports drink, FinHalsa high-protein bars, dried fruits, trail mix and Fig Newtons. Bob admitted to me, "We'll be drinking things you can't even spell."

On October 10, 1991, the pedal boat team in the newly named *Spirit of Moët* met at the South Street Seaport for a departure ceremony that featured the 200-year-old Napoleonic art of "sabrage." Using a razor-sharp twenty-four-inch military saber, the Moët & Chandon representative deftly sheared the top of a champagne bottle with surgical precision. Champagne geysered everywhere.

Bob told the well wishers gathered on the pier, "To put the physical side of the trial run in proper perspective, each of us will do the equivalent of a marathon in the morning, followed by another in the afternoon, and then repeat this feat for six days in a row." He told the crowd that everything was roughly timed each day around their pedaling routine—they carved up each twenty-four-hour period into single-pedaling, double-pedaling, and sleep periods.

The gathering of friends, relatives, and the media was dutifully impressed as they watched the odd-looking craft, a cross between a submarine and a sailboat without a mast, head to sea.

I nervously followed their progress by phone as they called in their position just off the southern shore of Long Island. In this modern era of instant communications and GPS navigation systems in the family car and on wristwatches, it seems almost quaint to realize that the best way to track their position back then was through status reports made by their brick-sized cell phone.

As they turned the corner at Rockaway Point outside New York, my staff dutifully wrote down their first message. The ocean was particularly rough, and Dwight reported the shake-down cruise was starting to give them both the shakes. "The seas quickly built to six feet with an occasional eight-foot wave that would slam into the pedal boat's beam, cascading spray into the air, not to mention that which entered the fore and aft ports. A few quick hands on the whale-gusher bilge pump, and all was dry inside."

During the nights they alternated two hours on, two hours off, keeping a watchful eye for commercial ships that could crush them in the blink of an eye. Temperatures ranged widely from 35 degrees to over 100 degrees Fahrenheit as they cruised along at approximately six knots (about seven mph).

They fought boredom by tuning their Sony Walkmans into the Clarence Thomas hearings on Capitol Hill. "Who would have guessed that we'd be listening to accounts of pubic hairs on Coke cans out in the Atlantic?" Bob remembers.

The 300-mile shakedown cruise took four days and twenty-one hours, nearly a day less than they had predicted despite stiff headwinds, strong tidal currents, driving rain, intense electrical storms, and rough ocean waves. The trial run demonstrated the viability of pedal-powered watercraft in heavy currents. It provided insight into the importance of nutrition to keep the team fueled—9,000 calories per person and over three gallons of various liquids per day.

The voyage to Boston also revealed the inadequacy of their bicycle sprocket-and-chain system—constant pedaling was eating away the sprockets. They decided that for the actual Atlantic crossing itself, they would switch to a more reliable belt system, similar to that on a motorcycle. "If we hadn't planned that shake-down, we would have been toast if the pedal system failed in the middle of the ocean," Bob said.

The trial run also revealed the importance of the medical research they were conducting. In fact, it was Bob's main rationale for devoting so much time and energy to the project. "The nutrition plan was bulletproof. It was stunning. The trial convinced me that this was infinitely feasible from a technical and medical point of view."

Yet despite some later support from Virgin Atlantic and Breitling, they found themselves the following winter unable to afford the chase boat that would have carried the enormous amount of food required to fuel themselves. Take away the escort boat, and the venture would have to cram all the food for the trip into the pedal boat itself. When Bob realized they could neither accommodate the added space nor the weight, he had no alternative but to drop out.

"The whole venture morphed into 'two men against the sea,'" Bob would recall years later. "The science element was really important to me. It could have been a fascinating story about using technology and planning to smash a human-powered record. But without the support boat, I couldn't rationalize continuing."

What was to be a team effort soon fell on Dwight's shoulders to accomplish solo. Friends and family were aghast. Was it a suicide mission? Or a valid attempt to demonstrate the extreme limits of human performance?

Dwight stripped out the tandem pedaling station, crammed the whole forward section with mostly freeze-dried food, and departed St. John's, Newfoundland, at 2:30 p.m. on June 14, 1992. A small crowd was there to watch as the former SEAL, firmly ensconced in his custom-molded orthopedic chair canted eleven degrees, pedaled furiously out of the harbor.

With his legs stretched out as if on a recumbent bike, Dwight pedaled solo for all his might. The hardest leg was during the first two weeks, Dwight remembers. Progress was hampered by constant head winds from the northeast and the frigid Labrador Current, at times two knots (about 2.3 mph) in opposition, he told Ebba Hierta in the October 1992 issue of *Soundings* magazine.

Dwight pedaled an average of 19.5 hours per day during the trip, sitting there in his hydrophobic, sweat-wicking sports apparel, energy bars and sports drinks at the ready.

"I was so driven, I didn't realize how bad I felt. I was just like a machine, doing what I had to do," he told *Soundings*. During one particularly depressing stretch, he covered a measly ten miles, according to an account by Amy Nutt in *Sports Illustrated*. But another time he managed to pedal ninety miles in twenty-four hours.

At times waves were up to thirty feet and winds reached gale force. Despite the rough ride, heavy weather helped slingshot him eastward. "By the end of the trip, I had gone through so many gales I could hardly keep track," he told *Sports Illustrated*.

He dodged trawlers, suffered major bouts of boredom when his Sony Walkman died due to moisture, and had a twelve-foot shark trail him for a few terrifying minutes. At times he donned a waterproof survival suit for protection. His only serious mishap occurred when a violent roll threw him out of his bunk across a beam, tearing a gash in his forehead.

Still, he told *Soundings* a few months later, "I wasn't incredibly lonely. It was my time to reflect on things. I'm one of those people who is always busy, all the time. I can't think of the last time I just sat and thought. It was a real luxury."

He would later tell me, "I wouldn't trade for anything those rare moments of connection to something far bigger than myself when I was by myself in the middle of the Atlantic Ocean."

Dwight arrived July 24 at 3:30 p.m. in Plymouth, England, forty days and about 2,300 miles later—the fastest human-powered west-to-east crossing of the Atlantic ever recorded. He blew away the previous record crossing, a fifty-five-day solo row set in 1987 by British oarsman Tom McLean. Dwight lost thirty pounds en route, in part because he strayed from the 7,000–9,000 calorie daily diet carefully designed by Dr. Steve

Johnson, head of the University of Utah Human Performance Research Lab and nutrition consultant to the U.S. Ski Team.

The British tabloids considered Dwight a madcap mariner obsessed with the call of the wild, someone who ". . . can't face life without proving his manhood." Harsh words indeed for someone who thousands of armchair adventurers vicariously followed each day.

Moët was thrilled. News of their involvement was covered as a sports story, as a general news item, and as a human-interest feature, reaching a cross section of their target market in the process. The brand received additional exposure when they arranged for an empty champagne bottle to be thrown overboard with a note inside offering the finder his or her weight in champagne. It was found four months later washed ashore in Brittany, France. A native Frenchman who stumbled upon it took the bottle to some English-speaking neighbors, and learned of his booty.

"Normally, we're featured on the wine pages or in the society column," the brand's Aura Reinhardt told *Industry Week*. "This gave us the opportunity to associate ourselves with journalists in other fields."

Dwight Collins, the man with the champagne taste in adventure, but the beer budget, can be gratified to know that the project is still being recognized. Today *Tango* hangs above Falconer Hall in the Maritime Aquarium at Norwalk in Connecticut. Educational displays and a video describe Dwight's experience and explain the technology involved in his unprecedented crossing, an adventure that attests to the importance of taking a test drive—in this case a shake-down cruise—before the start of any adventure.

Become Media Savvy

Climbing a mountain, pedaling across the Atlantic, or racing across Death Valley pushing a baby jogger full of food and water—that's the easy part. What's really hard is keeping sponsors happy. One way to do so—and this may sound elementary—is to credit corporate benefactors during media interviews. Easier said than done. As hard as you try to mention your sponsors, the media will try just as hard to cut them out. After all, their job is to inform, not sell. Reporters don't want to hear you plugging every cash and in-kind sponsor. The key is to narrow the field and credit those top two or three sponsors that have provided the most support.

When the Coleman Company provided support to Denver schoolteacher Mike Haugen for his expedition to Mount Everest, we spent hours advising him on how to deal with reporters.

We told Mike to listen for openings that would allow him to mention Coleman as naturally as possible, letting the company name flow almost as an afterthought. We told him to take the keys and drive the interview.

When you find yourself in the limelight, and your sponsors are expecting at least a mention of their company or brand, listen for these openings:

Q. How did you support yourself on the expedition?

A. Companies such as Coleman and brands like Gore-Tex and CW-X believe in what we're doing and have provided funding.

Q. How does a pedal-boat adventurer pay the bills?

A. It's difficult without corporate sponsorship. That's why we depend upon the support of Moët & Chandon.

Q. Tell us about plans for your next expedition.

A. We just signed a sponsorship agreement with LEKI USA for trekking poles.

Q. How is the fundraising going?

A. Thanks to thousands of donations on our Web site and funding from Coleman, Du Pont, and 3M, we've raised $100,000, but we're still seeking contributions from the general public.

Q. How does this trip compare with the expedition 100 years ago?

A. Technology makes this a different trip from Admiral Peary's 1909 expedition. For one thing, our Apple laptops will allow us to communicate directly with schoolchildren.

Q. What will conditions be like in Antarctica?

A. We expect the weather will be brutal, which is why we've worked closely with Coleman to request Exponent Siege dome tents with weather-resistant fabric and a wind-responsive frame.

Q. How long have you been working on this expedition?

A. Literally months. We needed to raise sponsorship dollars and determine the best outdoor products for the trip. For instance, instead of down sleeping bags, which are useless when wet, we found that bags containing synthetic insulation like Du Pont Quallofil work best.

Media training exercises with a friend assuming the role of reporter will help you nail these interviews cold. Imagine Matt Lauer of the NBC *Today Show* or Harry Smith of the CBS *Early Show* asking the questions. How would you respond? How would you deliver a memorable interview while at the same time expertly weaving in identification of one or more sponsors?

Finnish sailing skipper Ludde Ingvall was a master at crediting his sponsor, Pharmacia and Upjohn, at the slightest prompt. The media swarmed over his sleek, high-speed eighty-foot sailing yacht *Nicorette* prior to Ludde's attempt in 1997 to break the speed record for a monohull sailboat crossing the North Atlantic, some 3,000 miles from Ambrose Light at Sandy Hook, New Jersey, to Lizard Point, England. Working with a public relations agency called CGPR in Marblehead, Massachusetts, I trained Ludde for a press conference at New York's Chelsea Piers and a *Today Show* appearance. If the words "Nicorette" failed to register with viewers, the entire public relations effort would be for naught. Thus, it was important to stack the deck in our favor with targeted media training for Ludde that focused on seamlessly integrating the yacht's name—which also happened to be the name of the sponsor's nicotine gum—into each interview.

But we weren't about to take any chances. Ludde also wore a green fleece-lined jacket branded with the Nicorette Big Boat Racing Team logo, had the boat's name printed in big, bold letters on the boom, and frequently explained how the sponsorship was compatible with the sponsor's anti-smoking crusade, which he considered "the most pressing health problem facing the world today."

Our media blitz kept Ludde occupied while he awaited fierce spring weather to slingshot the boat to Europe. It was a great story: here was a sailing crew actually praying for bad weather, the kind of major low pressure system normally associated with snow storms, floods, and hurricanes, to help them break a ninety-two-year crossing record of twelve days, four hours, one minute. "Bad weather for you is great for me," he told the *Today Show* audience.

Finally, as the barometer began to fall like lead ballast, the moment came for the boat to depart New York Harbor, aided by a young and enthusiastic crew of fifteen from nine countries, high-tech satellite communications gear, and a 6,000-square-foot spinnaker, main, and headsails made with fibers stronger than steel and lighter than silk. Despite some harrowing moments, it all came together for the team, their anxious sponsor, a public relations team biting their nails down to the first joint, and Ludde, who took to calling himself "Captain Chaos." The *Nicorette*, powered purely by sail and the sweat of her crew, finished over 14½ hours faster than the previous record holder, the 185-foot three-masted schooner *Atlantic* in 1905.

"We sailed our hearts out and made history," we quoted Ludde in a Nicorette press release. "This crew has become a real family, and I am proud of every one of them. We experienced eighty-knot gusts, a whale who had a mind of its own, boredom, exhilaration, and highs and lows, but we persevered and achieved our dream."

Crew member JB Braun of Marblehead, a sailmaker by trade, would later remember one particularly horrifying thirty-six-hour storm. Speaking to Michael O'Connor of the *Boston Herald*, he reported how thirty-foot battens, which help stiffen the sail, began to shatter and fly away in seventy-five knot (eighty-six mph) winds. "We were afraid the shards would come down and slice right through us like spears, but the wind was so strong, they just flew out to sea."

Braun continued, "On the deck, it was just madness. The wind was always howling. And I mean, you couldn't say, 'OK, I've had enough, let's head back to shore.'"

To make matters even worse, the shrieking weather was driving them closer to ice fields in the North Atlantic. They decided to remove all the sails after a 100-mph jolt just about knocked them over, according to the *Boston Herald* story.

A final independent analysis of the press coverage revealed the project generated 902 million media impressions in four targeted countries—the United States, United Kingdom, Ireland, and Sweden. This came to an equivalent advertising value of $9.2 million, far more than the cost of the sponsorship itself. Ludde's Nicorette Big Boat Racing project went on to complete a total of thirteen years of partnership (until 2005), as well as winning two World Championships (1997 and 1999) that generated enormous exposure for the Nicorette brand. It became one of the longest-running promotions in the sport and the kind of return on investment any sponsor would love.

Prepare for the Trip of a Lifetime

Start Training—Himalayan Mountain–climber John Roskelley of Spokane, Washington, who summited Everest in 2003 with his twenty-year-old son Jess, has said of climbing, "If it isn't on television every weekend, it isn't a sport. Look at most of your high school and college athletes: as soon as they get out of school, you'll find them fattening up on a bar stool drinking beer. Climbers can't afford to go to pot. You're not risking the Heisman trophy up there, it's your life."

One well-known trainer of climbers and other adventurers recommends you start with the correct attitude. Dave Wahl of Athletik Spesifik Sport Performance in Thornton, Colorado, feels there is a difference between people who are motivated to achieve success versus people who are motivated to avoid failure. "The success-oriented people are willing to fail to become successful versus the other group that doesn't try hard enough to ensure the avoidance of failure," he advises. Dave uses physical preparation as a catalyst to become mentally tough.

When training, Wahl's clients are instructed on classic freeweight lifts integrated into a circuit that includes various gymnastic exercises such as push-ups, pull-ups, and dips with a leg raise.

A third exercise group that complements the circuit involves explosive strength or power exercises. These can be tuck jumps, clapping push ups, ladder drills, telemark hops—all exercises to incorporate speed and power into the system.

Wahl's last category is what most people think of as "aerobic," but when done in a circuit, blurs the line between aerobic and anaerobic. A treadmill, stationary bike, and a jump rope can all be incorporated into the circuit for greater physical and mental toughening.

"If you are unsure of your technical execution, seek help," he advises. "You can't pursue your travels with an injured back, and you can't get stronger if you're injured" (athletikspesifik.com).

Want Credibility?—Join the Club

THE FASTEST WAY TO GAIN EXPERIENCE IN ADVENTURES AND EXPEDI-tions is to hang out with the right kind of characters. One way to do that is to consider joining one of three main organizations in the field.

The Explorers Club—Founded in 1904, this is the country's preeminent exploration organization. As such, it's open to men and women who demonstrate credible contributions to field research, scientific exploration, and educational dissemination of that knowledge. Be fair warned: there are strict criteria for becoming a member. The Club and its approximately 3,000 members make a distinction between the eco-tourist or traveler and the explorer-scientist who contributes new knowledge for the benefit of others. To join, you need to have gotten your hands dirty and feet wet in the field, and secured recommendations from two current members. Regardless of whether you have the credentials, you can become an associate member, which allows you to attend events, but not vote or hold office. It is seen as a stepping-stone to eventual full membership, especially if you become chummy with members who invite you on one or more of their expeditions.

The Club is located in an urban version of a classic English manor house built in 1912 on Manhattan's tony East 70s. Exhibits of priceless explorabilia include a globe said to have been used by Thor Heyerdahl when planning his famous Kon-Tiki Expedition, an Arctic supply sled from Sir Hubert Wilkins' 1928 expedition, Club flags that have gone into space, and artwork from the late 1920s used to create backgrounds for the American Museum of Natural History. But it's the Trophy Room that most visitors ask to see. This sixth-floor lair harkens back to the days when mighty explorers would not only observe wild beasts, but shoot, ship, and taxidermically display them back at the Club, the perfect setting for regaling fellow members with their daring accounts.

A larger-than-life painting of Danish explorer Peter Freuchen (1886–1957), which has gazed down upon the Trophy Room for years, is the stuff of legend. The imposing full-length portrait by Robert Brackman was designed to show off the explorer's wooden leg, which replaced the one amputated in 1926.

For visitors to the Club, the story of Freuchen is almost as memorable as the nearby whale phallus (a sight that prompts some cheeky Club members to sniff, "Seems a bit small to me").

Club legend has it that the big-boned, six-foot seven-inch Freuchen escaped entrapment in a frozen tent on Baffin Island by fashioning what one might indelicately call a "shit knife." According to *Peter Freuchen's Adventures in the Arctic* (Julian Messner, 1960), the explorer created a partial hole in the snow/ice with a bearskin, but it was not big enough for him to climb through. He tried, and his beard stuck to the sled runner and froze to it. When Freuchen yanked his head back, his beard stuck and ripped skin off his face. Soft snow then filled the hole. As he lay trapped in his snow tomb, he remembered that sled-dog excrement froze solid as a rock.

Freuchen writes, "Would not the cold have the same effect on human discharge? Repulsive as the thought was, I decided to try the experiment. I moved my bowels, and from the excrement I managed to fashion a chisel-like instrument which I left to freeze. This time I was patient; I did not want to risk breaking my new tool by using it too soon. At last I decided to try my chisel, and it worked! Very gently and slowly I worked on the hole...."

Earlier, when he suffered severe frostbite and gangrene on his left foot, he knocked off the toes with a hammer. Doctors later amputated his left leg. Explorers Club members are nothing if not resourceful.

I've been a member since 1989 and have met some of the world's leading explorers there, from Sir Edmund Hillary and Buzz Aldrin to John Glenn and Sylvia Earle. My most memorable evening occurred while promoting the Club's "Space Dinner" in 1992. Afterward I shared a cab crosstown with the late astrophysicist Carl E. Sagan, PhD.

There I was, sitting next to one of the greatest minds of the late 1900s, and all I could think to ask was, "What's up with that 'billions and billions' catchphrase?" With a slightly amused look, Dr. Sagan told me he never said it; it was originally a Johnny Carson bit that over the years was accredited to Sagan himself.

The signature event of The Explorers Club is its annual dinner at the Waldorf-Astoria in New York. In fact, it's said to be the oldest continuous fund-raising dinner in the city. Highlight of the ECAD, as it's called, are the exotic hors d'oeuvres served during the cocktail hour.

Explorers are a hardy bunch often called upon to make enormous compromises, especially when it comes to food, or what passes for food in remote regions of the world. In many places on the map, insects offer a lion's share of dietary protein, carbohydrates, fat, vitamins, and minerals. There's even a scientific name for chowing down on bugs: entomophagy.

The Explorers Club delights in serving such ghastly fare, along with wild boar, ostrich egg canapés, curried Tibetan ram, alligator, sea cucumber, duck tongue, vertebrate optic globular capsules (eyeballs), and some creepy crawlies usually seen only on reality TV.

Yet, contrary to what you might expect, within an hour the tables are picked clean. Exotics chairman Gene Rurka is not surprised. "Eighty percent of the world's population savors insects. They can be used as delicacies or as staples of everyday diets. High in nutritional value, some insect species contain as much as 60 percent protein with only 6 percent fat per 100 grams, approximately one-quarter pound. Sure beats hamburger, doesn't it?" he tells me.

Well, not really. I'm adventurous, but not that adventurous when it comes to insects roasted, poached, boiled, sautéed, or stir-fried. What's more, normal fare like hamburgers and french fries usually doesn't require action from the New York City Health Department. In 2001, dinner bit back. City health officials nervously called for the recipe after receiving a number of complaints about burning and numbness among guests that had scarfed the tempura tarantula in ponzu sauce. Seems tarantula hairs on the abdomen and legs were creating an allergic reaction. There could be millions of us allergic to tarantula hair, although most of us might prefer never to find out. One year later, farm-raised tarantulas were back—200 strong—hairs fully singed and marinated in Jack Daniels. If you didn't grab one quickly you were out of luck (explorers.org).

The American Alpine Club—The AAC, founded in 1902, is dedicated to inspiring and supporting the climbing community, and protecting its playgrounds around the world through conservation and advocacy. The AAC is perhaps best known for publishing the world's most sought-after annual climbing publication, the *American Alpine Journal*; caring for the world's leading mountaineering library; and offering annual climbing, conservation, and research grants to budding adventurers.

The AAC looks out for its members by providing them with a global rescue service and the annual "must read" of climbing disasters called *Accidents in North American Mountaineering*, edited by Jed Williamson. It includes such heart-warming topics as rappel errors, fuel bottle explosions, strandings, falling rocks, tumbling falls resulting from glissading with crampons, and unexplained disappearances. If this fifty-year-old classic source of climbing-related accidents doesn't dissuade a climber entirely, it will at least help increase his or her likelihood of climbing safely. Just in case, the book includes a directory of Mountain Rescue Units in North America.

The AAC is headquartered at the American Mountaineering Center in Golden, Colorado, in the same historic building as the new Bradford Washburn American Mountaineering Museum, which the Club helped establish. The museum is named for the late cartographer and mountaineer from Boston who died at the age of ninety-six in 2007 after an amazing career that saw Amelia Earhart attempt to enlist him as navigator on her ill-fated around-the-world flight. He declined because he thought the radios were inadequate; obviously it was a smart move. Washburn is also remembered for directing an expedition that remeasured Mount Everest seven feet higher.

Within the museum is one of the most historic artifacts in the world of mountaineering, a single ice axe that saved the lives of five men—a single piece of climbing equipment that has since come to represent the pinnacle of mountaineering ethics.

According to the museum, the year 1953 was a great one for mountaineering. By its end, the summit of Mount Everest was achieved. Austrian Hermann Buhl climbed alone to the summit of Nanga Parbat in Pakistan to become the first person ever to complete a solo first ascent of an 8,000-meter peak (26,247 feet).

However, on K2, the world's second-highest mountain, a saga unfolded that has forever remained etched in the annals of mountaineering. The tenacity and strength displayed by the members of the expedition team remain legendary.

A storm on the Abruzzi Ridge—at an altitude of 25,300 feet on the slopes of K2—sent climbers led by Charles S. Houston, a doctor from

Seattle, scrambling to save the life of a fellow mountaineer. Climbing alpine style without the aid of oxygen, team member Art Gilkey's left leg was stricken with thrombophlebitis and began filling with blood clots. He would die if a clot were to reach his lungs. With no other option than to transport Gilkey to a lower elevation as fast as possible, the team began to maneuver him down the precariously steep and icy slope in his sleeping bag, in the middle of a vicious storm. Team member George Bell suddenly lost his footing and, in the ensuing entanglement of ropes and climbers, five men started plunging toward their deaths off the face of the mountain.

The youngest and strongest man on the team, however, would keep this expedition from being remembered solely for its tragedies. Moments after Gilkey, still sedated with morphine in his sleeping bag, and the other five men began sliding to their deaths, a chemist from Seattle, Pete Schoening, instinctively jammed his ice axe in the snow behind a small boulder. This impromptu rope belay—with the rope wrapped around both his hip and the wooden shaft of the axe—resulted in a quick-thinking arrest that prevented the five men from almost certainly perishing.

Unfortunately, Gilkey would later be swept into the void by an avalanche at the age of twenty-seven. . . . Or perhaps he released the ropes himself in an act of self-sacrifice to protect his teammates. No one will ever know for sure. Nonetheless, Schoening's life-altering act has since defined the expedition. "The Belay" is now recognized as one of the most heroic acts in mountaineering history.

The five climbers saved by Schoening in Pakistan that day went on to resume their lives and raise families—the "Children of the Belay" they're called, according to Karen Molenaar Terrell, the daughter of dangling expedition member Dee Molenaar. There are more than thirty descendants of the original team alive today because of Pete Schoening and his axe (americanalpineclub.org, bwamm.org).

Royal Geographical Society—The Royal Geographical Society, established in 1830 to promote the advancement of geographical science, supports research, education, expeditions, and fieldwork, as well as public engagement and informed enjoyment of the world.

The London headquarters of the RGS is housed in one of the city's most important examples of nineteenth-century architecture with its red brick, rubbed and cut brickwork, and irregular but balanced compositions in the Queen Anne style. The place literally reeks of history. Walk down a hallway and come face-to-face with a priceless map of the world on Mercator's projection dating to 1608. Turn a corner and you'll find a section of the tree from Central Africa beneath which the heart of Dr. David Livingstone (of "Dr. Livingstone, I presume?" fame) was buried in a tin box in 1873.

A number of resources are available to research an upcoming project: a fully-stocked library, map room, and archives containing over 5,000 reports with details of the achievements and research results of expeditions to almost every country in the world. There's also a database of another 8,000 planned and past expeditions dating to 1965 covering a wide variety of sporting, scientific, and youth expeditions.

Members can take advantage of the Expedition Advisory Centre (EAC), which offers regular training workshops and seminars for more than 500 teams annually. The EAC also runs the popular Explore Expedition Planners' Seminar. Attend this annual November conference, and it becomes evident that while it's no longer true that the "sun never sets on the British Empire," it's a safe bet that at anytime of day or night, there's a British explorer studying something somewhere. At Explore, upwards of 200 current and would-be explorers gather to compare notes and network. Whether the seminar is about the spread of jigger fleas in rural northwest Cameroon, studies of the remote island caves of southern Chile, or a "Grease to Greece" journey to Athens in a biofuel truck, there's no better place to see the legacy of wandering Brits like Robert F. Scott, Ernest Shackleton, and Dr. David Livingstone come to life.

One lad at the 2008 conference walked around with a sign taped to his back that read, "I want to go from Ward Hunt Island to the Pole. Will you help?" Other attendees posted bulletin board notices seeking partners to travel around North America, to Everest, through the Amazon, and even to Mars. It's worth the trip to London just to attend (rgs.org).

Back to School: Where to Get the Knowledge and Experience You Need

☞ **Learn the Ropes**—Sign up for outdoor courses to learn specialized skills that will come in handy in the wilds. AMC Outdoor Explorations, for instance, part of the nonprofit Appalachian Mountain Club, offers instruction ranging from short, one-hour skills clinics to multi-day guided adventures. There are workshops in whitewater and sea kayaking, rock climbing, dogsledding, llama trekking, GPS orienteering, and even one that helps you identify scat left behind by different animals (certainly helpful if you wonder whether it's a mountain lion or a harmless whitetail deer you're hiking behind). Geology, mountain ecology, and weather study are some examples of the natural history classes available.

During the cold-weather months, learn snowshoeing, cross-country skiing, winter hiking, ice climbing, and more. At the Joe Dodge Lodge at Pinkham Notch in the White Mountains of New Hampshire, you can take AMC courses in avalanche awareness, wilderness first aid, and winter mountaineering. Then come back on Memorial Day with your skis or snowboard, hike 4½ hours up to Mount Washington's Tuckerman Ravine, and take a few runs with the crazies who have made skiing Tucks a late-season tradition (outdoors.org).

☞ **Take a NOLS Course**—Refine your leadership skills, take the trip of a lifetime, or prepare for a career in outdoor education by enrolling in a course offered by the National Outdoors Leadership School (NOLS). Since 1965, outdoor enthusiasts have come to NOLS to learn the skills they need to climb mountains, run rivers, and even ski backcountry powder (in which case, count me in). People of all ages go on wilderness expeditions, and learn outdoor skills, leadership, and environmental ethics in some of the world's most awe-inspiring classrooms. The NOLS hands-on, learn-by-doing approach means graduates learn to become competent, responsible wilderness travelers. Of particular interest is one of the pillars of the NOLS leadership curriculum: expedition behavior (EB), which focuses on being able to live with a group of people 24/7, to serve the mission and goals of that group, and to be as concerned for others as you are for yourself. The organization's Wilderness Medicine Institute defines the standard in wilderness medicine training when 911 is not an option, resources are scarce, there is no help on the way, and you have to make your own decisions. A NOLS course will help even up the odds a bit in your favor (nols.edu).

☞ **Certify Your Mountaineering and Climbing Skills**—If you already have strong outdoor skills, you can become certified by the American Mountain Guides Association based in Boulder, Colorado. Certainly, it would demonstrate to sponsors that you've got the goods. Since the early 1990s, the AMGA Accreditation Program has focused on international standards for climbing, mountaineering, ski guiding, and instruction. Certified individuals also benefit from a Pro-Purchase program that offers discounts and special promotions from over fifty manufacturers to certified individuals. What's more, a financial aid program provides more than fifteen scholarships per year to qualified applicants seeking training and certification (amga.com).

☞ **Become a Citizen Scientist for Earthwatch**—For almost forty years the Earthwatch Institute has relied on volunteers to support global research programs with their money and time. Consider volunteering as a research assistant alongside leading environmental scientists and local conservationists as they pursue vital field research. In 2009 you could choose from among 350 expeditions on sixty research projects in eighty countries. There are studies of leatherback sea turtles in Trinidad, whales in British Columbia, dolphins in Greece, the mammals of Nova Scotia, and Alaskan fur seals, to name a few. Expeditions range from Very Easy (must be able to walk one mile per day) to Strenuous (involves hiking up to 15 miles per day carrying equipment up to forty pounds). It's a win-win situation—scientists benefit from desperately needed volunteer assistance as you gain valuable experience that may help you someday snag a sponsor for your own future project (earthwatch.org).

Make the Pitch

"Who is this guy?"

"Why is he calling so often?"

"Why does he think he deserves our support?"

You may think your project is as good as the one launched by Christopher Columbus, but potential sponsors will most likely beg to differ.

Is the search for someone to pay for your dream trip difficult? Unquestionably, unless, perhaps, you can find your name on the Forbes 500 list. The process of soliciting funding can be daunting, even if your name is Shackleton. In fact, especially if your name is Shackleton.

Sir Ernest Shackleton (1874–1922), the British polar explorer, wasn't the Shackleton we all know today when he started out, hat in hand, pitching sponsors. It would take years before he gained renown as the Great Polar Pitchman.

Shackleton was considered by biographer Roland Huntford "an eloquent, brooding, magnetic, half-poet, half-buccaneer, possessed by romantic visions and intense ambition."

He hungered for the South Pole, "the last spot of the world," as he put it, "that counts as worth the striving for though ungilded by aught but adventure." Little did he realize his polar quest would lead to a historic rescue mission that was a triumph of the human spirit over great adversity.

Shackleton served under Commander Robert F. Scott on the Discovery Expedition (1901–1903), then led his own British Antarctic

Expedition in 1907–1909, reaching within a record ninety-seven miles of the South Pole and discovering the South Magnetic Pole. Shackleton was feted as a national hero and knighted by Edward VII. Still, he was constantly dogged by financial difficulties. While achieving worldwide acclaim for traveling "furthest south," he still faced the daunting task of paying off his debts and raising funds for his next expedition.

Shackleton believed Antarctica held promise as the path to fame and fortune. Among explorers, he was the only one who openly promoted his expeditions as a commercial venture, according to Huntford's book, *Shackleton* (Atheneum, 1986). Funding would result, he was sure, from telling the story in books, lectures, newspapers, and cinematographs (movies). To raise money, he lured investors with the promise of another Klondike—a source of minerals and precious stones.

By granting advertising rights, he received a free motorcar to reach the South Pole, despite the fact that the automobile was notoriously un- reliable even in the best of conditions.

He auctioned off news and picture rights to London newspapers, even earned money by writing jokes for a Fleet Street publication. He turned his expedition ship, the *Nimrod,* into a museum and charged ad- mission, according to Huntford. Special postage stamps were sold with a cancellation mark from the Antarctic. A handsome, charismatic speaker, he went on a 20,000-mile lecture tour reading poetry and recounting his exploits using fragile glass lantern slides and a film, the first shot in Antarctica. An Antarctic mountain was named after *London Daily Ex- press* journalist and *Punch* humorist Sir Henry Lucy to curry favorable publicity. Shackleton was also believed to be the first polar explorer to produce a phonograph record. Not surprisingly, he landed a book deal, wrote about his previous expedition, and no doubt was thrilled when it was published in nine languages.

Shackleton's skills as a fund-raiser eventually allowed him to depart Plymouth, England, on August 8, 1914 aboard the *Endurance* for the Trans-Antarctic Expedition, the first-ever attempt to cross the Antarctic continent. While trying to reach the continent, the *Endurance* became frozen in an ice floe deep within the Weddell Sea and drifted with the pack for ten months before being sunk by crushing ice in November 1915.

Man-hauling the ship's three lifeboats, Shackleton and his party of twenty-seven men sledded across the ice for nearly 200 miles to reach open water and then sailed to deserted Elephant Island, where they landed in April 1916. After setting up a small camp there, Shackleton and five other men braved the freezing ocean in their twenty-foot lifeboat, the *James Caird,* on an 800-mile journey to find help. Upon arrival at South Georgia Island in May, he and two of the men crossed twenty-four miles over a 6,000-foot mountain range to reach Stromness, a whaling station on the opposite side of the island.

Shackleton's arrival at the station manager's office was legendary, says Carmen Field, a writer for Zegrahm & Eco Expeditions based in Seattle. In her well-researched account she tells of a Norwegian who remembered (in somewhat broken English) "The Boss," as Shackleton was called, and his two comrades stumbling in. "Everybody at Stromness knew Shackleton well, and we very sorry he is lost in ice with all hands. But we not know three terrible-looking bearded men who walk into the office off the mountainside that morning. Manager say: 'Who the hell are you?' and terrible bearded man in the centre of the three say very quietly: 'My name is Shackleton.' Me—I turn away and weep. I think manager weep, too."

Shackleton returned to rescue the twenty-two members of his party who were living a bleak existence, sleeping beneath overturned boats on Elephant Island. Not a single life was lost. It was, according to the *New*

York Times, a "glorious failure—perhaps the most astonishing survival epic ever told."

Shackleton died of heart disease in 1922 at the early age of forty-eight and lies buried, at his wife's request, on South Georgia Island near the whaling ghost town of Grytviken.

Remember the story of Sir Ernest Shackleton when it seems as if every potential sponsor has suddenly lost your email address and telephone number. Sure, it's difficult to shake the money tree. But it has always been tough. Your alternative? Pay for everything yourself, just like the late adventurer Steve Fossett, who had the means to self-fund his various projects.

If you're in need of funds for your project, the spirit of Admiral Richard E. Byrd feels your pain: "I have never known an explorer who was not either bankrupt or close to it," he famously said.

After the Lion's Rock caper with John Roskelley, I became involved in adventure marketing almost full-time starting with a phone call in 1984 from Will Steger, another explorer who would latch onto a sponsor prospect like a pit bull and never let go.

Will, a wiry dogsled musher and adventurer from Ely, Minnesota, was desperately looking for sponsorship. Du Pont had a budget to promote the product performance of sleeping-bag and parka insulation, and Will wanted some of it to lead the first confirmed and unsupported dogsled expedition to the North Pole.

Deceptively low key and as thin as a pole, Will would come to Du Pont headquarters in Wilmington, Delaware, practically starving. He would encourage them to take him to lunch so that, short on funding during those early days, he could engorge himself on the meal, likely his only one for the day.

Carol Gee, my agency contact at the company, remembers his 1985 visit to the company's Wilmington headquarters. With his belt cinched too tight for a hotel room, Will arrived with nothing more than a backpack and a promise. "I looked at this small guy . . . and I said, 'I bet he'll do it,'" she told Mike Cannell of the *New York Times*. "There was something about him. A gleam in his eye."

After lunch, he would spread his huge Arctic map on a conference room table. The suits, myself included, would dutifully rise and peer at its topographic lines intensely. It's as if the adventure came alive right before our eyes. Will had us hooked as he proceeded to charm the company out of tens of thousands of dollars. But reeling in Du Pont took substantial effort. The chemical giant's executives were more accustomed to sponsoring golf or tennis tournaments than extreme adventures. At least no one froze to death on the back nine, they reasoned. But a North Pole expedition? It would require a major leap of faith for an otherwise conservative company. This was an organization that took safety so seriously that the speed-limit signs at plant entrances in Wilmington read 24 MPH because research showed they would be more memorable one mile per hour lower than twenty-five.

At the end of that pitch meeting, Will relayed to the *Times*' Mike Cannell that Gee told him, "I'm going to get the check for this if it's over my dead body." She raised $25,000 in cash and products within Du Pont by touting Will's planned trial run—a 5,000-mile solo dogsled trek to Point Barrow, Alaska—as a demonstration that synthetic-fiber sleeping bags, when wet, still retain warmth better than down bags.

The dogsled trip to Alaska was also a way for Will to prove his mettle. Leading his team was Zap, whom we dubbed the "publicity hound." We shamelessly paraded Zap around New York with a Du Pont cape on his back. It was the polar version of Budweiser's Spuds Mackenzie. Zap, who had his own reservation at the New Yorker Hotel, would later gain renown when his penis froze en route to the North Pole; Will, happily, avoided the same fate and would go on to become America's greatest modern-day polar explorer.

Will launched his fifty-five-day Steger North Pole Expedition in 1986, financed by a combination of cash and gear from over sixty companies, including proceeds from official expedition T-shirts reading, THE CHOSEN FROZEN and ZAP TO THE POLE. The expedition would become the first confirmed and unsupported dogsled journey to the North Pole, with an emphasis on the word "confirmed," since historians to this day aren't absolutely sure whether Peary was first to the North Pole (although they are convinced both he and Frederick Cook came close). Of course, Cook's credibility wasn't enhanced by his conviction for mail fraud in 1923, followed by seven years in Leavenworth Federal Prison.

When it comes to raising money for your dream trip, no single sponsor is likely to be your Oliver "Daddy" Warbucks. More likely, funding will come from a variety of sources, as it did for Will Steger, or later, for Colonel Norman D. Vaughan of the Mount Vaughan Antarctic Expedition, who would take money from anyone, anywhere, anytime. When Norman was short of funds, which was, truth be told, a constant state, he and his staff got creative. He received funding from Kohler Corp., makers of toilets, and MACE Corporation, makers of chemical MACE spray, who sent in tens of thousands of dollars. Norman sold bandanas, coffee mugs, and shirts at the Alaska State Fair, and had numerous in-kind sponsors. Grabber Warmers supplied the entire team with chemical heat packs for their hands; Cascade Designs provided mattresses.

Local TV stations donated airtime to sell the expedition's imprinted merchandise. Over 4,000 letters were sent to area businessmen asking for donations. The local telephone company sent out bill stuffers with information about Norman's project, and he opened a storefront in an Anchorage shopping mall. His local health club sponsored a benefit fund-raiser, and they even had two salespeople selling commemorative coins door to door.

The Kindness of In-Kind Sponsors

In the search for someone to pay for your trip, first start by requesting cash. Don't spend the first six months of fund-raising begging for a free pair of socks. First of all, you can't go wrong with cash. It comes in the right color, is easy to use, and is extremely portable.

Eventually, depending upon your level of success, you'll want to consider defraying your costs with donated gear, or a combination of cash and gear. You'll find that outdoor companies are more willing to become sponsors through gear and apparel donations because it represents soft dollars for them, especially if it comes from excess inventory. Cash, if they even have a budget at all, comes to you kicking and screaming, with a lot more strings attached.

While in-kind assistance can't help fund everything, it can go a long way. The North Face donated $200,000 in specially designed clothes and tents to Will Steger's 3,741-mile Trans-Antarctica project. As you'll see below, in-kind sponsorship allowed one team to travel as many as 150,000 miles.

A New York journalist and her photographer husband came to embrace in-kind sponsorship as the best way to launch their project.

Karen Catchpole and her husband Eric Mohl, both in their early forties, had one of those adventure ideas that could be written on the back of an envelope: leave their jobs, get in a truck, and drive 150,000-plus miles to twenty-three Western Hemisphere countries in under four years. The plan was to try to visit more than 850 national parks, preserves, and wildlife sanctuaries, 136 UNESCO Biosphere Reserves, and a number of state, provincial, and regional parks and reserves in North, Central, and South America.

They were hopeful that magazine and newspaper editors would be clamoring for the next great adventure story. Karen, an editor herself, spent three years as senior editor of *Jane* magazine, and now freelances for major travel publications. In fact, she was one of my strongest media contacts, once even traveling on a press trip we organized to test drive Volvos and learn to fly fish at Orvis in Vermont. I'd often visit her office at *Jane* with one or more clients in tow for deskside presentations. Unbeknownst to me, she had been spending three years planning the trip of her dreams—especially scheming how to pay for it.

"As we roam from the Arctic to Tierra del Fuego, through the Rockies and the Andes, to Mount Rushmore and Machu Picchu, we will use skills and contacts developed over twenty years in journalism and photography to sell and place stories in U.S. and international consumer magazines and newspapers," she told *Expedition News* before departure.

In April 2006, Karen and Eric, unencumbered by children or mortgages or other financial responsibilities that shackle most of us, embarked on their Trans-Americas Journey (trans-americas.com) in a sponsored Chevy Silverado 1500. Things were going well until twelve months and almost 50,000 miles into their journey. It March 2007, Chevy abruptly pulled out of the partnership and asked that they return the vehicle, blaming the change on their legal department, which was becoming cranky about loaners lasting more than a year. Karen suspected that a new head of the Chevy communications department was suffering from NIH Syndrome—"Not Invented Here."

"It seemed like he simply didn't want to spend any time or energy working on a project that wasn't his idea," Karen said, advising, "Lesson learned? Get it in writing."

The two had left jobs and an apartment in New York City believing they had a solid vehicle partner for the full three- to four-year journey.

When Chevy let them down, they pulled off an end run, receiving a substantial discount on the purchase of a 2007 Chevy Silverado 2500 HD from a dealer in Little Falls, New Jersey.

Karen says, "When we first started seeking support for the Trans-Americas Journey back in late 2005, we were primarily asking for money. But no one we approached had the budget for cash sponsorship no matter how interested they were in the Trans-Americas Journey.

"So we quickly shifted gears to what we call 'product partnerships' and that has been much more successful for us and crucial to the project's budget."

Karen and Eric avoided misunderstandings or misplaced expectations by providing each potential product partner with a detailed proposal that spelled out what the Trans-Americas Journey was, who they were, exactly what they were seeking from the company, and what they were willing to offer in return.

Companies that provide products with more value were offered more sponsorship benefits in return. For example, a smaller-dollar-amount product partner might be offered the use of one brief testimonial and a photo of the product in use on the road. A more substantial product partner was Airstream, which joined in June 2008 with the loan of a 2008 Airstream twenty-three-foot aluminum Safari Special Edition trailer to pull behind the Chevy for six months.

In return, Karen and Eric agreed to write an Airstream Adventure "Travelogue from the Ultimate Road Trip" blog that they updated with text and photos roughly three times a week (transamerica.airstream.com).

After a time, the need for cash sponsorship somewhat lessened. New in-kind sponsors included Adventure Medical Kits, Amsoil, BF-Goodrich, Bilstein, Cocoon, Costa del Mar, Dell, KINeSYS, KOA, Mile

Marker, Mountainsmith, Optima, Pacsafe, PIAA, point6, Silver Joe's Coffee, SteriPen, Superchips, Surefire, and Weather Guard. It's a meaty list, one that any budding adventurer would do well to note.

They also learned to be flexible, creative, and willing to work with a company to modify their proposal when necessary. For example, Columbia Sportswear could not (or would not) commit to either a cash sponsorship or full product partnership, but they did give the two access to low-cost apparel in their employee store in Portland, Oregon, and through their Pro Purchase program for outdoor industry insiders. "It was not exactly what we were hoping for, but every little bit helps, and we were grateful for it," Karen said.

"Simply not having to purchase all of the gear, truck components, gadgets, etc., that have been given to us has saved almost $20,000, which was substantial to a project like ours.

"Now if we can only get a fuel partner . . ."

You have a choice when it comes to paying for your trip. Either pay for it yourself, or seek outside funding. The first approach may well drive you deeply in debt, just like it did history's greatest explorers, but it's certainly an option. After all, preparing sponsorship proposals, visiting prospective funders, creating a logo, and establishing a Web site—it all costs money.

"Who needs it?" asks explorer Felicity Aston, of Birchington, England, speaking at a 2008 conference at the Royal Geographical Society.

"You're better off reducing the size of the expedition and, if you need to, holding your own fund-raising events. If you're not prepared to pay for an entire expedition by yourself, then why should your sponsor?" In 2006, Aston led the first team of British women across the Greenland ice sheet,

and in 2008 traversed frozen Lake Baikal in Siberia with used and borrowed gear and a miserly budget of £3,000 (about $4,500 at the time).

If mushing your way deeper and deeper into debt does not sound
particularly attractive, remember that if you convince someone else to
pay for your project—preferably a big, fat corporate sponsor—there's a
trade-off. Unless the money is an outright gift, you need to return value
to your sponsor—publicity, product evaluations, appearances at sponsor
events, and so on—all explained in your sponsorship proposal in exacting
detail. The more a sponsor pays, the more benefits you should be prepared
to deliver. Creativity plays an important role as well, as I'll explain.

What Sponsors Want

☞ **Title Sponsorship**—Mushers say that unless you're the lead
dog, the scenery seldom changes. Be prepared for sponsors that want
to be top dog—companies that insist you call the project the (Name
Of Company) Mount Everest Expedition, or (Your Name Here)
Sahara Desert Expedition. How's this for a mouthful: the Vaseline
Research Everest '94 Expedition? Be willing to compromise on the
name of the project: the funding could make all the difference between an expedition that breaks even and one that breaks the bank—
your bank. Savvy sponsors know it's often better to be title sponsor of
a smaller expedition than one of many supporters of a larger one.

Admiral Robert E. Peary was well aware that the wealthy businessmen he was pitching to support his North Pole expedition would
want to see some return on their investment. A solicitation he mailed
in the early 1900s glowed with promise: "And if I win out in this
work, the names of those who made the work possible will be kept
through the coming centuries floating forever above the forgotten
and submerged debris of our time and day."

☞ **Bragging Rights**—Far down the sponsorship food chain are companies that merely want bragging rights and are willing to provide little or no cash, but plenty of in-kind support—gear and clothing, for instance, that you'd have to purchase anyway. One climb offered sponsors a low-cost opportunity to participate through its "Bak a Yak" program. Donors were charged a fee to place their company logos on the side of a sweaty beast in the Himalayas.

☞ **Cause-related Marketing**—Select a nonprofit organization to support, one that can provide a "halo" around your corporate sponsors. Through its sponsorship of Will Steger, the Shaklee Corporation, a nutrition company, basked in the glow of good corporate citizenship as they promoted awareness of the environment and helped educate school children who followed along. It also gave them a perfect opportunity to send newspaper and radio/TV editors "edible press kits" containing samples of the vitamins, energy bars, and powdered soup mix that it supplied to explorers.

☞ **Visual Identification**—Savvy sponsors want to see their corporate logos everywhere—on your dogsled, kayak, clothing, headwear, you name it. Think of auto-racing signage, and you get the general idea. The more a sponsor pays, the larger the logo. It's that simple.

☞ **Photo/Video Rights**—Sponsors will want to have either exclusive rights to images and video, or more likely, shared rights. Both the sponsor and you have the right to use your videos and images in advertising, Web sites, sales-collateral materials, and other ancillary uses.

☞ **Category Exclusivity**—If Coke sponsors your trip, don't think you can also accept money from Pepsi. Sponsors become a bit crazed when they have to share the limelight with competitors. Also, make sure your team members avoid making their own side deals with competitive products.

☞ **Product Evaluation**—Offer to test new products in the field, where performance can be a matter of life and death. Be prepared to present a written analysis of the product—a stove, a lantern, or new parka, for instance—to the sponsor's Research and Development department. John Roskelley, one of the world's best-known alpinists, told Gordon Wiltsie in *Outside Business* magazine that while sitting out a storm in a tent in the Himalayas, "I watched icicles dripping from the roof onto my [sleeping] bag, and right through the sewing-needle holes. But next to me, the [liner] shell stayed dry. Later, Eddie Bauer incorporated my input into a more consumer-oriented three-season bag that proved to be one of their best selling models."

Wiltsie agrees, "If a mountaineer feels a cold spot in his sleeping bag, or if his boots cause blisters, and the manufacturer is able to correct these problems, consumers will get a product that is well worth the few extra dollars."

☞ **Personal Appearance Days**—Guarantee a certain number of days during which time you will be available to the sponsor for personal appearances. These include retail store visits, public speaking engagements, media interviews, plant tours, trade show visits, or all of the above. Adventurers and explorers often go on sales calls. When the time comes for a sponsor to present a new outdoor clothing line, for instance, what better endorsement than from someone who staked his or her life on the garment?

☞ **Customer Entertainment**—Some sponsors will find value in building rapport with their top retail buyers by having you guide mini adventure trips. Suggest ways sponsors can become closer to their key customers, whether it's a fly-fishing trip, a climb up Mount Rainier, or a dogsled outing.

In addition to these standard off-the-shelf benefits, you'll endear yourself to a sponsor by getting creative, really creative. Think of ways to tailor the project to a sponsor's specific needs, providing value they never dreamed possible when they first opened your pitch.

Consider the story of the Steger North Pole Expedition "Polar Capsule."

During a training trip to Baffin Island, just prior to Will Steger's historic 1986 North Pole Expedition, I spied a piece of PVC pipe the team left lying on the snow-covered ground. Orange on one end, with a white screw-on cap at the other, it was about five inches circumference and two feet long. It looked like any other sewer pipe you might find in your basement, but for the Steger project, it had special meaning. The team planned to fill it with expedition memorabilia, then leave it at the North Pole when they arrived that spring. When the frozen ice cap broke up for the summer, they were sure it would either sink or float away.

For me, this wasn't a sewer pipe, it was a "Polar Capsule," an opportunity to generate additional publicity for the expedition and its major sponsor.

I convinced Du Pont to offer a $5,000 reward for the capsule's safe return, knowing full well that it would cost many times that amount for someone to charter a plane and retrieve it from the Pole, assuming it didn't first sink or float south—which is the only direction it could travel from the Pole. When he sealed the capsule and tossed it over an ice ridge, Will's coleader, Paul Schurke, was sure he would never see the capsule again. Du Pont was confident its money was safe.

Skip ahead almost three years. I'm at the International Events Group conference in Chicago, and I receive an urgent call from my staff to contact the office. The National Geographic Society had called to say they received a letter from Peadar Gallagher, an Irish carpenter who was taking an afternoon stroll along the rocky Atlantic shore near Bloody Foreland Point, 150 miles northwest of Dublin, and approximately 2,400 miles from the North Pole. He stumbles across the capsule, unscrews the top, and out pours Polaroid snapshots with "National Geographic" written in pen. Weeks go by before he contacts the American Embassy in Dublin, which suggests he send an inquiry to the National Geographic Society headquarters in Washington, D.C. More weeks pass before the Society puts two and two together, and contacts Will's expedition office in St. Paul, Minnesota. Will's people waste no time in calling us.

My hands are shaking, I'm so excited.

"What? The Polar Capsule? Where, when?" I shout into the phone.

Days pass and I finally call Gallagher and offer to pay his way to The Explorers Club in New York to pick up his reward and meet the press. For good measure, I throw in an offer for first-class travel.

He will have no part of flying anywhere. I can't believe it. I call his brother on Long Island, call Gallagher again, plead by mail, but he won't budge. He says if we want the capsule we can bring him the money and pick it up personally.

Plans for an international press conference in New York are looking grim when we convince a Du Pont executive in London to schlep to Gallagher's home and hand the recalcitrant carpenter the money. With capsule in hand—actually in the Du Ponter's carry-on lest it become lost baggage—the capsule is personally flown to New York for presentation to The Explorers Club.

Much of the contents are destroyed. Remaining intact is a Minnesota Girl Scout troop flag, a Polaroid of the team taken at the North Pole, and a ten Kroner bill. Unfortunately, a scroll containing the signatures of the expedition members and approximately 200 supporters is waterlogged beyond recognition.

No matter, the recovery of the capsule fascinates the country. The Associated Press runs the story, and soon it appears in hundreds of newspapers, providing a huge return on Du Pont's $5,000 investment.

Remember when planning your trip, it may look like a sewer pipe, even smell like a sewer pipe, but if positioned creatively could be a golden opportunity for your sponsor.

How To Secure a Sponsor

☞ **"Wow" 'Em**—"Your expedition needs a USP—a Unique Selling Proposition—to encourage people to say 'Wow!' when you explain it," says London-based Neil Laughton, an entrepreneur, aviator, and adventurer who holds paraglider, hang-glider, paramotor, fixed-wing, and helicopter licenses. A Seven Summiteer who climbed the tallest peak on each continent, he was the first person to jet ski around the U.K. and holds world records for extreme golf, Tin Tray Racing, and even the Twenty-Four-Hour Pram Pushing Record.

Laughton suggests explorers under-promise and over-deliver. That's exactly what he accomplished when he helped make a wish come true for a disabled athlete in a wheelchair, whom he led to Everest base camp. After arriving at the top, they climbed an adjacent peak. "Don't be shy—ask potential sponsors what they want to receive from your expedition. Meet them eye-to-eye so they can share in your passion," he said.

Will Steger's former expedition manager and fund-raiser, Cathy de Moll, agrees. She told Mike Cannell of the *New York Times* to find someone in a company who shares the project's vision. "If you can find that person—it doesn't matter what he does in the company—he'll find a way for you." Of course, the closer to the executive suite you can get, the better.

☞ **Keep It Short**—Prepare a short, concise proposal. No one has time to read long emails or bother with high-resolution attachments, especially outdoor-industry sponsors who complain of being inundated with yet another sponsorship proposal every time they log on. Keep it brief and stay focused: What do you want to accomplish? Where are you going? Who are you? And what benefits will the sponsor receive?

☞ **Practice Your Elevator Pitch**—When potential sponsors ask you about your project, they're not looking for a long, drawn out song and dance.

"I'm going to fish the roadless areas of the Pacific Northwest."

"I'm golfing across Mongolia."

"I'm going to be at sea for 1,000 days without ever docking."

Keep it short and sweet. They want to know what time it is, not how to make a watch.

If you don't know the sponsor contact, and it's your first approach, embed the pitch within the email, not attached. Pay attention to that subject line. Remember that the first few words count most as your prospects may be reading the short subject lines that appear on their BlackBerrys or iPhones.

By the way, spelling counts. As you'll later read, one explorer who wrote to *Expedition News* wanted to go on an "expidition." Enough said.

☞ **Market Professionally**—Finding a sponsor is a full-time, sixteen-hours-a-day job, explorer Paul Schurke told writer David Butwin in *Northwest Orient* magazine. Tasked with raising $150,000 in supplies, services, and funds to support the 1986 Steger North Pole Expedition, Schurke said of the challenge, "It was no different for

Peary in his day. It's the old dog-and-pony circuit. We put on our furs or our business suits and go knocking on a thousand doors."

A thousand doors? It's best to obtain the services of an assistant, a dedicated Web site, email, and telephone. Have the assistant run a "torch and spark" operation to churn the waters by contacting fifteen to twenty new sponsorship leads a week, then send a short email, followed later by a more detailed email and a request for a meeting. This assistant "sparks" interest, sending out a blizzard of solicitations, so that you can go in to light the "torch"—spread your map out on that boardroom table, and land a sponsor.

☞ **Check Your Supply List**—Will Steger's North Pole Expedition had a list of over forty separate equipment items, from MSR stoves and REI carabiners, to Olympus and Canon cameras, to Eveready batteries—gear he needed to successfully run his expedition. A few years later, for the Trans-Antarctica Expedition of 1989–90, Will knew they needed a special kind of long underwear that would trap body heat and wick moisture. Team members tried Du Pont's Thermax, which contained a unique hollow-core fiber that mimicked the fur on a polar bear. Their success with the product led Will to once again approach the company for support.

Will then pitched Hill's Pet Products when he realized his supply list called for an astounding 25,000 pounds of dog food. He traded the food for sponsorship rights and twelve days of personal time for promotional appearances.

One year, sailing legend Dennis Conner came to us for help in preparing an America's Cup sponsorship request to Du Pont. Dennis had figured out how dozens of products the company makes—including Kevlar fibers and Dacron polyester—sat literally within an arm's length of the helm. He considered Du Pont products as much a part of his team as his tactician and port/starboard grinders. In fact, each Du Pont executive at his pitch meeting received a small cross-section of a *Stars & Stripes* hull mounted on a wood block. It was a simple memento that would remind them of their meeting with the first man to lose the America's Cup and the first to win it back.

Create a target list of prospective sponsors based upon everything you plan to take along. Then convince the company that their product plays an integral role in the success of the project. One Web site that will help you determine what you might need is gearjunkie.com, which is devoted to the outdoors, health, fitness, adventure travel, and all the gear and equipment associated with those pursuits.

☞ **Target Adventure-friendly Companies**—Corporations that use adventure imagery in their print ads or TV commercials already understand the value of adventure marketing. Rolex is one that immediately comes to mind, but there are dozens of others. For sponsorship leads, review the advertisers of adventure magazines such as *National Geographic Adventure, Men's Journal,* or *Outside.*

☞ **Secure Media Coverage in Advance**—Sponsors want to know that their support will eventually be credited in the media. Your project becomes infinitely more marketable if you have a commitment from a magazine, TV program, or newspaper that will run a story about your exploits. According to the *Royal Geographical Society Expedition Handbook* (Profile Books, 2004), this is easier said than done. "If the publication cannot sell advertising on the back of your expedition piece, and you are not a famous explorer, the story has to be extremely strong, as well as being well written and original."

To decide which magazine or newspapers to pitch first, review appropriate target publications by buying them on the newsstand or visiting the periodical section of your local library. As for adventure TV programs, watch TV, check local listings, then Google the Web site of each show for contact information.

☞ **Consult Target Lists**—Consider buying lists of sponsors from the International Events Group. IEG issues the annual *Sponsorship Sourcebook,* which connects more than 6,000 sponsors, opportunities, agencies, and suppliers (sponsorship.com).

Nielsen Sports Group creates a directory of up to 1,200 outdoor gear and apparel manufacturers who exhibit in Salt Lake at the Outdoor Retailer Winter Market or Summer Market trade shows (outdoorretailer.com).

Another approach is to purchase the O'Dwyer's Directory of Public Relations Firms. It identifies 9,500 corporate clients at 1,900 public relations agencies, many of whom are likely sponsors of your project. If anyone understands the publicity value of an adventure sponsorship, it's a company's public relations agency (odwyerpr.com).

☞ **Timing Is Critical**—Start your corporate outreach effort well in advance of need. July of the previous year is not too soon, since many companies work on their next year's marketing budgets during the previous fall. On the other hand, there's an off chance that companies will have money left in their budgets that they need to spend by year's end. Some may even be looking for fire sales—projects that are willing to drop their sponsorship fees dramatically days or weeks before departure.

☞ **Work the Old Boy (or Girl) Network**—Create an email list of everyone you know who can do you some good. Make it viral: ask them to pass your solicitation to others. Issue periodic updates to keep everyone in the loop on a regular basis. Set up a Facebook page and send out frequent updates to your online friends.

☞ **Make a Personal Pitch**—There's nothing like a face-to-face meeting. Attempt to visit potential sponsors in their offices, or during the major trade shows they attend. The aforementioned Outdoor

Retailer trade show is a good place to begin. Gearheads come to drool over the latest products from companies such as LEKI, Mountain Hardwear, Patagonia, Sierra Designs, The North Face, and about 800 others all under one roof. The show is so outdoor friendly that dogs are allowed to attend with their owners. While closed to the public, it's possible to purchase a pass for about $400–$450, or better yet, convince a friendly local retailer or exhibiting manufacturer to add you to his establishment's registration list.

☞ **Solicit Charitable Donations**—What's the best way to solicit charitable donations for your upcoming cause-related project? There is no best way. Funding needs to come from a variety of sources. The more creative you are, the greater your chances of success. The Web site climbupsokidscangrowup.com, which is running the Mount Kilimanjaro climb mentioned earlier, has a section containing fund-raising advice, from soliciting everyone you know, to organizing garage and bake sales, setting up donation canisters, raising money through eBay and Facebook, and soliciting support from local gyms, schools, radio stations, hair salons, churches, bowling centers, and book stores. Don't forget fraternities, sororities, and alumni organizations as well.

Picture This

T HE IMPORTANCE OF PHOTOGRAPHY TO ANY ADVENTURE OR EXPEDI-
tion goes back to, well, almost the dawn of photography.

Creating a record of the Robert F. Scott expedition aboard the *Terra Nova* was the responsibility of photographer Herbert George Ponting (1870–1935), a pioneer in the use of photography as an art form. In 1909, when Scott appointed him "camera artist" to the expedition, Ponting became the first professional photographer to visit Antarctica.

His work on Scott's 1910–12 expedition is arguably considered, quite simply, the finest photography ever made of an expedition. Surely, the stills and motion-picture film footage, which immortalized Scott's final expedition, must have been in their day the equivalent of taking an IMAX camera to the top of Everest. They are among the most enduring images of polar exploration.

In "Ice Cave," Ponting's most famous image, the camera captures two explorers at the mouth of a cave with the *Terra Nova* in the far distance, framed by a fringe of long icicles. "The Castle Berg" was the most beautiful iceberg seen by the expedition and resembles a medieval castle. "Chris and the Gramophone," which evokes the famous RCA logo, shows a Siberian husky intensely listening to a phonograph recording of a lecture by Admiral Robert E. Peary titled, "How I Reached the North Pole."

Ponting was forever persuading members of the expedition to pose. Scott even invented a new verb: "ponting," or "to pont," meaning "to pose until nearly frozen in all sorts of uncomfortable positions." Ponting, however dedicated, never made it to the South Pole. Scott said his "Southern Party" could not transport Ponting's heavy apparatus because every ounce of space was needed for food.

Just months after his death in 1935, Ponting's entire collection of glass-plate negatives was sold by his son for about $120 to help pay off his father's debts. Today a single image taken by Ponting can easily command upwards of $25,000.

How did modern-day explorers become interested in exploration? I've heard over and over that they can trace their wanderlust to reading *National Geographic* when they were young. Will Steger told the St. Paul *Pioneer Press Dispatch* that his interest in the Poles was sparked as a young boy when he traded outgrown hockey skates for a wagonload of magazines.

By taking its cameras into the field, *National Geographic* brought archaeology, the arts, science, and adventure into people's homes. To this day, polar explorers, South Pole scientists, and cruise-ship passengers visiting Antarctica wear red parkas because the color is said to show up best in color magazine photos.

Photography is the single best tool for providing value to sponsors. Where media coverage fails to credit sponsors in the text itself, you can compensate through careful placement of sponsor patches on apparel and accessories such as hats and gloves; banners on dogsleds, canoes, and mountain bikes; and logos on tents and support vehicles.

The challenge is to walk that fine line between providing sponsors with the visual ID they crave and appearing as if you were a NASCAR racer covered in logos from head to toe. Studying photographs of expeditions in this book and on the Web will help determine what's appropriate and how not to turn into a walking version of Times Square. Generally speaking, sponsor patches need to be at least six square inches and positioned in the vicinity of the forehead or collarbone to have the best chance of pick-up. When one athlete crossed the Atlantic on a sailboard, the Nestlé Crunch logo was placed on his wetsuit over his throat, gaining ID for the sponsor in newspapers worldwide.

One look at media coverage generated by Will Steger's Trans-Antarctica Expedition in 1989–90, and it becomes apparent who sponsored it. There are bold Gore-Tex and UAP logos on parkas, located high over the collarbone to make it tougher to crop; because of their lower financial commitment, Du Pont Thermoloft identification was placed on less visible shoulder patches. Rugged mountaineering tents carry logos from The North Face, while Target, in a $1 million deal as official retailer of the Trans-Antarctica Expedition, branded a customized forty-eight-foot traveling exhibit that toured store locations and schools.

During some adventures or expeditions, team leaders brush up on their photography skills in advance, then shoot their own images once in the field. The iconic 1953 image of the first man to summit Mount Everest, assumed at first glance to be Sir Edmund Hillary, is actually his climbing partner, Tenzing Norgay, simply because Hillary had the camera and knew how to use it. Shortly afterward, meeting a team member during his descent, Sir Edmund would refer to their first ascent in his understated New Zealand manner, "Well, we knocked the bastard off."

Often it's best to leave photography to the professionals, preferably a "shooter" experienced in the outdoors, someone who feels comfortable even in extreme conditions.

My go-to guy has long been Gordon Wiltsie, part photographer, part climber, part mountain guide. This modern-day Ponting runs a thriving photography business in Bozeman, Montana, and supplies adventure images to advertising art directors, magazine editors, greeting-card designers, and photography galleries.

For thirty-five years, Gordon has produced images for nearly every outdoor and climbing magazine in the business, including cover stories for *National Geographic,* and is passionate about photographing vanishing cultures around the world. He is a former participant of over one hundred expeditions—often for five to seven weeks at a time—on climbing treks to Antarctica, dogsled expeditions in the Northwest Territories, and journeys through China, sometimes blending in as a team member himself, carrying loads, making camp, cooking, mending gear, and performing other daily chores.

He works best when every member of the group understands what is required to capture the right images—whether it's an early morning wake-up call to catch the sun, or late afternoon "magic hour" photo session. Frequently you'll find him ahead of the group to photograph the sense of discovery from an unusual angle or perspective.

Needless to say, Gordon understands the difference between machine-gunning massive numbers of individual images, and the importance of that one single image—a signature photo—that says everything about an expedition.

On behalf of sponsors 3M Thinsulate LiteLoft, Shaklee, and Lands' End, I commissioned Gordon to accompany Will Steger on a training expedition for his International Arctic Project in 1994. We needed one image for *USA Weekend* magazine that symbolized what the expedition was about. Somewhere northeast of Tuktoyaktuk, an Inuit village on the coast of the Arctic Ocean in Canada's Northwest Territories, he positioned Will Steger in his tent, lying inside a sleeping bag entering the day's activities into a journal, while a sled dog sat patiently outside. It had all the elements we needed: The Thinsulate logo was clearly visible, and the picture would eventually be seen by millions.

Was it an artificially contrived photo? Indeed it was. But it was certainly better than the travesty Gordon wrote about in *Outside Business* magazine. In the article he told of one veteran climber who reported that over twenty years ago during an Antarctic expedition, "The cameraman needed a shot that really said 'Antarctica,' [so he] made the rest of us get out on the ice, catch penguins, and tie their feet to stakes so they couldn't get away. The only problem was that sometimes the parachute cord showed around the penguins' ankles."

Neither of us would suggest trying that today.

～◌～

It's one thing to capture an image in the field, and quite another to transmit it back home almost instantaneously to a waiting audience of armchair explorers. Today anyone can link their digital camera to a satellite telephone from the most backwater regions of the planet, then onto the Internet. But it wasn't always that easy.

I pushed technology to the edge in October 1995 when I hired a Brooklyn-based news photographer named Mark D. Phillips to photograph a tightrope walk—to this day history's longest and highest—across China's Qutang Gorge, the most spectacular of the fabled Three Gorges. But the word "tightrope" doesn't do it justice. Listen to former circus performer Jay Cochrane, a thin, intense, milk-drinking athlete in his sixties with impossibly orange-blonde hair, and he'll tell you it was a high-wire "skywalk." Listen to my father, a retired but still savvy menswear retail consultant from Seventh Avenue, and he'll say, "Schmuck! You have a tightrope walker for a client? Better get your money up front!"

Jay, nicknamed the "Prince of the Air," became a client when he was looking to promote his plans to walk 2,098 feet, some 1,340-feet above the Yangtze River. The Chinese hired the wirewalker to bring international attention to the Three Gorges Dam, the largest of its kind ever constructed, and deflect some of the criticism for the many cities and towns that would be inundated. We brought in Mark Phillips because we needed an image of the feat, and we needed it fast, sent by telephone modem to the closest wire service. Easier said than done. Base camp was Fengjie, a historic city in southwest China's Chongqing Municipality about to be submerged by the dam.

First we needed a signature photo. One image that would communicate death-defying heights, an exotic location, and just one man, one wire, and a forty-five-foot balance pole. Mark stationed himself on the far end, waiting for Jay to complete his fifty-three-minute crossing in front of an estimated 200,000 Chinese spectators, and another 200 million watching on television across the country. Photography is all about access, being in the right place at the right time, so Mark spent two weeks scouting the best position for himself and his camera equipment.

Scrambling down to a narrow ledge, just below Jay, below the supports for the unforgiving 1¼-inch braided steel wire rope spanning the gorge, it was now or never. He fired off dozens of frames of film with his Nikon F3. When Jay simultaneously lifted one hand and one foot, we had our money shot.

Mark raced back to his room in a seedy hotel, developed the film in water that housekeepers boiled for him, and dried the color negatives with a hair dryer. He placed the color negatives into a scanner, then tried to secure a clear open telephone line to Agence France-Presse in Hong Kong. The transmission over the hotel's single long-distance circuit continued to crash. Finally, after sitting on his hotel-room floor attempting to connect for four hours, he managed to complete one seventeen-minute transmission. AFP distributed the image worldwide, and Jay made it into the record books.

Mark believes his digital transmission was one of, if not *the* first from an independent photojournalist sent from this rural region of the country. "It was at the cusp of digital photography," he remembers.

Mark would later become embroiled in controversy when a photo he took of the 9/11 disaster, an image shot from the rooftop of his Brooklyn home, seemed to show the face of Satan in the smoke enveloping the World Trade Center. The photo was sent worldwide over the news wires, and a media frenzy ensued when it began appearing on front pages nationwide. Mark was accused of doctoring the image for private gain, but was eventually vindicated when Olympus technicians verified the authenticity of the digital image. It was a case of pareidolia, the same phenomenon that makes people believe they can see the face of Mother Teresa in a cinnamon bun.

Get the Shot

☞ **Learn Photography or Hire a Pro**—Learn as much as you can about photography and be sure to become familiar with your camera in advance of the trip. If budget permits, hire a pro, preferably one with outdoor skills. Otherwise, at least read a book such as Bill Hatcher's *National Geographic Photography Field Guide: Action and Adventure* (National Geographic, 2006).

It is still a tall order to expect to master the art of photography overnight, no matter how good a digital camera you can afford. Above and beyond good exposure and focus, the intangibles are what matter most: the hard-to-define storytelling elements of what you put into a frame, and what you leave out. Gordon Wiltsie advises that the latter can be just as important as the former. The vital thing is to think "story." Why are you taking the picture? Does the image explain why you have undertaken a quest many rationally minded people might consider insane?

Wiltsie says William Graves, the former expeditions editor at *National Geographic* (and later the editor in chief), used to tell his protégés that expedition photography might be the most difficult venue of all because it so often means hauling out your camera when that is the very last thing that you want to do.

Gordon can attest to that.

"While I was with Will Steger at the North Pole in 1995, we experienced a real crisis shortly after the media crew for the International Arctic Project departed and we continued mushing south, back toward Canada. We didn't make it an hour before team member Martin Hignell's sled broke through thin ice, and I was torn by a dilemma," Gordon admitted years later.

"If Martin's sled sank any further, his dogs and everything on his sled would go two miles to the bottom of the ocean. How could I not feel morally obligated to forget photography and to help Will, Martin, and everyone else to pull on the traces and salvage the situation? But what did Will yell at me? 'Take pictures!'"

Gordon continued, "I traded off on my responsibilities, and—thanks in part to experience, I think—finally captured a picture that turned out to be the opening spread of the expedition's *National Geographic* story. It was also the 'signature image' of the entire trip—you can even see Will yelling at me to 'shoot,' with another team member pulling with all of his strength."

☞ **Fiercely Protect Your Images**—I tend to become fairly compulsive when it comes to protecting valuable images, going so far as to keep one set on my camera's digital memory card, one downloaded to my laptop, and another set on a DVD. Former Explorers Club president Richard Wiese suggests downloading images to a portable hard drive, such as the 160 GB Epson P-7000, which also doubles as a multimedia photo viewer with a four-inch screen. "That way you can share the day's images with team members at night," he said. "I have used this on the North Pole, an Everest Expedition, the deserts of Ethiopia, the deepest canyon in the world in Peru, and on Kilimanjaro, without any type of failure."

☞ **Keep a Camera Handy**—Always keep your camera right at hand. Famed mountaineer and aerial photographer Bradford Washburn says in his book, *Bradford Washburn: Mountain Photography* (The Mountaineers Books, 1999), "Some of my best pictures were accidents or just plain luck. My negative 4481, 'After the Storm, Climbers on the Doldenhorn,' is just such an example. . . . I told the pilot to make a very tight turn and I got the shot, one of the best I've ever made."

Gordon Wiltsie agrees, "The best moments often come completely by surprise. You have to be ready to grab and shoot within seconds. A good expedition and/or adventure photographer can pull off a sequence of pictures with virtually no waiting time for anyone else. That readiness can mean everything for your sponsors who are depending upon you for great images they can use later on."

One low-tech solution to keeping a camera at the ready is a neoprene stabilizer strap by Op/Tech. Your hands remain free while the neoprene attaches to the camera's existing neck strap to hold the camera close to your body.

☞ **Keep Video Simple**—When it comes to video, try to keep it simple, advises the Royal Geographical Society's *Expedition Handbook* (Profile Books, 2004). "Straightforward shots of landscapes and events, with plenty of close-ups of people, are more usable by the media than footage riddled with pans, zooms and jazzy effects."

One excellent place to hone your filmmaking skills is at the Serac Adventure Film School, led by Michael Brown, who has directed films that have won more than forty international film festival and industry awards. He has summitted Mount Everest four times and was the first to bring an HD camera to the top. You'll gain hands-on experience in some of the world's most picturesque locations. Past trips of expedition teams of eight to ten people have visited Machu Picchu, Kilimanjaro, and the Colorado Rockies (adventurefilmschool.com).

☞ **Take a Climbing Photography Class**—*Rock and Ice* magazine holds an intensive four-day Photo Camp in Colorado's scenic Ragged Mountains that will improve your photography techniques, develop a more creative eye, and even help you gain insider knowledge about selling your images. The course, which will be helpful for any outdoor adventure, covers composition, critical lens selection, maximizing available light, digital in-camera tricks, and strobe lighting. Instructors include regular contributors to *National Geographic Adventure* and other leading outdoor magazines (rockandice.com).

Engage the Media

Why does someone decide to pursue a career in the media? It's certainly not because of the job security or the money. Sure, some reporters—think of Bob Woodward—can make a fortune if their probing investigations turn into books or movies. But most members of the media are in it because they like to tell stories. They like to have experiences that most people can only dream about.

I became fascinated with journalism at Syracuse University, where as a reporter and photographer for the campus newspaper, the *Daily Orange*, and reporter for an alternative weekly called the *New Times*, I had extraordinary experiences. I photographed a young Sen. Edward Kennedy, Jane Fonda, and John Lennon. I interviewed Rod Serling and the Woodstock Festival's Max Yasgur. I wrote investigative stories about a missing student named Karen Levy, and the shoddy construction of student housing. I visited a casket factory, spent a deathly dull night with a New York Thruway toll collector, and wrote a first-person account of my life as a Catskills resort bar waiter.

Reporters love to be part of the story. They love to experience an adventure themselves. Think how you can encourage the media to drink the Kool-Aid and experience a taste of what your project is really like. This technique has been a key part of our public relations strategies.

It is the winter of 1987, and I'm shivering overnight on a frozen lake. No tent. Certainly no bathroom. Just me in a sleeping bag, my assistant Jennifer Kimball some ten feet away, a few members of the press, and, oh yeah, the world's most experienced polar explorer, Will Steger. Prior to this, roughing it for me was a hotel without heated towel racks. But here I am with my game face on, the public relations representative from Du Pont, sleeping outside in minus twenty degrees Fahrenheit.

Chilling with Will is the longest night of my life. I'm in the Superior National Forest west of Ely, the virtual icebox of Minnesota, and I am shivering in spite of all the great attributes and product benefits associated with Du Pont Quallofil sleeping bag insulation.

Rewind back a year to when this frigid nightmare began. Will called me one day after Du Pont had sponsored his 1986 North Pole Expedition and said, "We'd like to invite the media to the Homestead.

"We'll take them on a dogsled ride, tell them about our upcoming expedition, even sleep outdoors," he promised.

Will was planning his next project, a seven-month, 3,741-mile non-mechanized crossing of Antarctica, and wanted the media to experience a sense of the hardship his team would soon face. He was thinking of entertaining writers, editors, and filmmakers somewhere cold and extreme, somewhere like his hand-built version of Superman's Fortress of Solitude located in the middle of nowhere.

Will's Homestead was a ramshackle 240-acre compound well off the grid near the Boundary Waters Canoe Area Wilderness, three miles from the nearest road. There were some hand-hewn cabins, including Will's two-room home crammed with books about polar history's leading men: Scott, Amundsen, Shackleton, and Peary. One partially finished multi-story structure was being built to eventually become the future home of a conference center. Then there were the dogs—what Will calls "polar huskies," well-loved, but mangy, rough-looking hybrids of Siberian husky, malamute, and timber wolf. Each has the spirit of a racer, the strength of a sled hauler, and the loyalty of a pet with romantic *Call of the Wild* names like Buffy, Panda, Choochi, and Zap Jr. The perfect temperature for these powerful, four-legged diesels is minus thirty to minus forty degrees Fahrenheit. When running, they can actually overheat at zero degrees Fahrenheit.

There were about forty sled dogs staked with tire chains to muddy A-frame plywood doghouses that reeked of dog piss.

"Don't pet them," I was warned by a staff member. "They'll knock you over and rip your arm off."

I backed away slowly, imagining life without an arm. Not pretty.

As part of their indoctrination, Will planned to feed his media guests pemmican, a staple of all polar explorations—a nasty paste of dried and pounded meat mixed with melted fat. It could clog the arteries of mere mortals in a heartbeat. But polar explorers crave fat when burning 6,000–8,000 calories per day as they travel from one camp to another.

So here I am, curled up in a sleeping bag, having a nightmare (during one brief period of actual REM sleep) that my body heat will melt a hole in the ice, I will fall through, and that will be that for the PR guy from New York.

But this outing isn't about me, it's about sharing with the media a sense of adventure. Sometimes you have to hit them with a two by four to have them pay attention to your project. There they sit in some busy newsroom. Emails are pouring across their screen by the minute, the phone is ringing off the hook, they're under a time crunch to meet deadlines, and their desks are piled high with press kits, free books, imprinted T-shirts, caps, stress balls, pens shaped like airplanes, and other tchochkes publicists seemingly purchase by the dumpster load.

Thus, if you can lure the media away from this morass and actually out to the field, get them to experience a dogsled ride, sleep in the sleeping bags you're peddling, or witness the magic of the northern lights, you create an advocate, perhaps a friend for life—a reporter, producer, editor, or freelancer as excited about the project as you are.

As far as Steger was concerned, no member of the media was more engaged than Jason Davis, a British Merchant Navy seaman and former cash-register salesman who became an Australian television news star. Eventually, he found his way to Minnesota and went on to produce thousands of stories about ordinary Minnesotans doing extraordinary things. If you were a schoolteacher who married a student sixty-eight years later, or a double amputee who scales McKinley, Jason would be there with a camera in your face. He's a Midwestern institution who, in 2008, celebrated his fortieth anniversary at KSTP with a special edition of his *On the Road* TV series.

Jason was there in 1984 when Steger set off on a 5,000-mile trial run by dogsled from Duluth, Minnesota, to Point Barrow, Alaska. He remembers the departure vividly in his book, *On the Road Again* (Voyageur Press, 1989), "It must have been the first time the dogs had heard of the plans for them to pull a sled five thousand miles, because the one on Will's left raised its leg and peed all over him. It wasn't exactly champagne, but it did get the training run off to a running start."

During his coverage of Steger's North Pole Expedition two years later, Jason told of weather so bone-numbingly cold, a quarter bottle of brandy left outside would freeze solid in minutes, and audio cables would become plastic-coated steel rods. He can still feel where his nose was so severely frostbitten it grew a bright white growth that demanded immediate attention or else he would have been taking his nostrils home in a Ziploc bag.

This was my first big project for Du Pont in the early 1980s. You'd never know John Roskelley, one of America's most experienced Himalayan climbers, was posing on a 30-foot boulder behind a New York restaurant. John doesn't look too concerned about free climbing it without protection.

There's a hidden engine, a life raft and some emergency radios on board, but otherwise the *Islendingur* looks as it would have one thousand years ago, minus, of course, 64 rowers.

A chase boat provided media with an opportunity to record the Viking ship's arrival as it sailed past the New York skyline.

Former WCBS-TV newsman Morrie Alter (holding microphone) joined the crew aboard the *Islendingur* as it sailed into New York Harbor. He was a master at telling stories—"little movies" he called them—in just three minutes.

Captain Gunnar Marel Eggertsson built this replica Viking ship practically by hand. It now sits in a museum outside Reykjavik that retells the story of the *Islendingur* and its commemorative voyage to the New World.

Susan Schurke (far left), and daughter Bria (second from right) were warmly welcomed when they arrived in Anadyr, in the extreme northeastern region of Russia, for the start of the Bering Bridge Expedition. Susan gamely agreed to wear a cap imprinted with the logo for Thermax thermalwear fabric, an expedition sponsor.

Following thirty minutes on the summit of Mount Everest in May 2007, Denver schoolteacher and Coleman spokesperson Mike Haugen would become involved in a life-or-death rescue.

Mike relied upon the performance of Coleman camping gear during his Everest and American highpoint projects.

Lindsay Danner, Mike Haugen, and Zach Price practically lived in this Toyota Highlander Hybrid SUV for 15,000 miles as the team broke the record for the fastest ascent of America's highpoints. I took this photo after they stuffed themselves silly with bacon and eggs at a local Darien, Connecticut restaurant.

There was no greater love than that between freedivers Pipin Ferreras and Audrey Mestre.

I shared a ride with Audrey on that fateful day in 2002 under dark, ominous skies.

The last thing Jennifer Kimball expected on her trip to the Arctic was to meet the man of her dreams, much less one wearing fur and carrying a rifle.

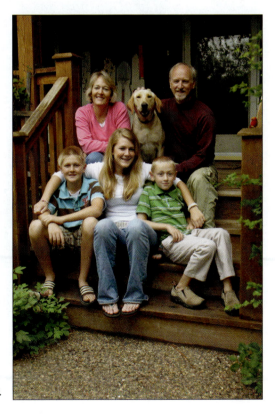

The Gasperini family at home in Minnesota. That's Will in the lower right, named for polar explorer, Will Steger, whose 1986 North Pole Expedition brought Jennifer and Jim together.

Dwight Collins (left) and Robert Wells of Connecticut were prepared to pedal across the Atlantic together until lack of funding eliminated the support boat that would carry supplies for two. Dwight proceeded to break the record alone.

Dwight Collins' strange-looking pedal boat before it was christened the *Spirit of Moet*, after his main benefactor. You can still see it hanging in the Maritime Aquarium in Norwalk, Connecticut.

Freelance writer Mike Finkel and I laughed our way through a Yellowknife, NWT, press trip. He's one of the most creative writers I know, with a love of the outdoors. Can't say much about his choice of cold-weather apparel, though. (right)

This is one of the friendlier sled dogs I've met. But these four-legged locomotives are not all this docile. (left)

As you go through life, there are people you never forget. Meeting and working with Colonel Norman D. Vaughan is one of the highlights of my career. That's Norman in front of his namesake mountain in Antarctica. (right) *(Photo: Gordon Wiltsie)*

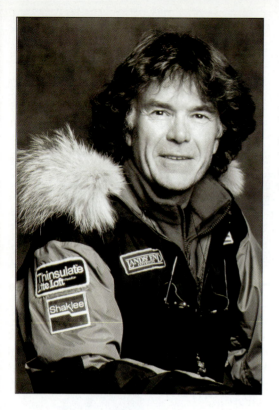

A publicity photo for Will Steger with each logo carefully placed for maximum impact. Visual identification is critical for delivering value to sponsors. The more exposure they receive, the more likely they will consider the next adventure or expedition request that comes along.

Expedition photographer Gordon Wiltsie carefully positioned Will Steger in this signature photo prior to an expedition across the Arctic Ocean. Special care was taken to ensure that the Thinsulate logo would be visible. Millions saw this image when it appeared in *US. Weekend.* Think this is an easy shot? You try getting a sled dog to sit still.

Ann Bancroft (third from left) read a statement to the world on May 1, 1986, when the Steger North Pole Expedition arrived at 90 degrees north latitude.

For Jason Davis of KTSP-TV in Minnesota, the colder the better. Frigid temperatures made some great images for television. He believes this report from Resolute was one of the earliest live television transmissions from so far north. The dish is pointed almost straight out to reach a broadcast satellite low on the horizon.

The Explorers Club is renown for serving exotic hors d'oeuvres, especially insects, at its annual dinner in New York.

Karen Catchpole and her husband Eric Mohl of the Trans-Americas Journey stickered up their truck to create additional exposure for in-kind sponsors.

Reid Stowe and his girlfriend and novice sailor, Soanya Ahmad, before pregnancy would force her to abandon ship.

It may look like a sewer pipe, even smell like one, but we decided "Polar Capsule" sounded a bit more adventurou: After he packed it with expedition memorabilia, Pau Schurke tossed it over his shoulder at the North Pole and promptly forg about it.

Peadar Gallagher, an Irish carpenter, found the Polar Capsule on the shore of County Donegal, Ireland, not realizing it was worth a $5,000 reward. It floated ashore from the North Pole three years and approximately 2,400 miles later.

It takes some chutzpah to ask skywalker Jay Cochrane to pose on one leg. But we needed a signature photo of his performance across Qutang Gorge and photographer Mark D. Phillips not only nailed the shot, but also struggled for four hours to email it to the rest of the world from deep within China.

One of over 400 homes covered in lava and ash when Heimaey, a small town off the coast of Iceland, was destroyed by a volcanic eruption in 1973. Volunteers are needed to help uncover some of the properties.

Jason and I later worked together on a project dreamed up by Minnesotan Paul Schurke, the coleader of Steger's North Pole expedition.

The city of Anadyr in the extreme northeastern region of Russia was a nightmarish collection of gray cinder-block buildings right out of the black and white episode of the *Twilight Zone* called "Eye of the Beholder," the one where ugly doctors operate on a beautiful woman while a totalitarian dictator blathers nonsense from TV screens.

Anadyr, a city of 16,000 people in the Chukotka district of the Russian Far East, was to be the departure point for Paul Schurke's Bering Bridge Expedition, sponsored in part by the Du Pont Company on behalf of a cold-weather fabric called Thermax. It was a natural tie-in since the material was made of hollow-core fibers that mimic the fur on a polar bear.

The story goes that for centuries, the natives of Alaska traded back and forth over the fifty-three-mile hourglass-shaped Bering Strait with their relatives in the Soviet Union. Even today, many Russian and American villagers in the Bering region speak the same language, share the same cultural heritage and, in some cases, are even related to each other.

With the onslaught of the Cold War, an "Ice Curtain" descended upon the region, restricting open travel between both sides of the strait. Fast forward to 1989—the Berlin wall comes crashing down, and travel restrictions slowly melt. The Soviets are thinking maybe "Glasnost"—the policy of openness and transparency—is the way to go.

Paul Schurke, then thirty-three, an Ely, Minnesota, neighbor of Will Steger's, hatches a plan: a two-month, 1,200-mile dogsled expedition linking communities in virtually roadless areas on both sides of the Bering Strait. The project would hopefully reunite family members separated by decades of mistrust between the two superpowers. This goodwill mission, an exercise in self-styled "adventure diplomacy," as Paul put it, promised to break the ice and help the locals rub noses for the first time in forty-one years. The Bering Bridge team would travel across a little-known area of the Soviet Union, becoming the first Western visitors to some villages in nearly half a century. From there, they would journey back across the turbulent waters of the Bering Strait and onto the western tip of Alaska.

It would be the first crossing of the central channel of the Bering Strait on foot since a mail carrier named Spike Milligrock, a long-time resident of U.S.-owned Little Diomede, made his way across in 1914.

Comedian Tina Fey famously parodied Alaska Governor Sarah Palin's comment about her ability to see Russia from her house. In these parts that's no joke. Russia's Big Diomede Island is located just 2½ miles from America's Little Diomede and is right there, in your face, on any clear day.

This proximity between the two superpowers is what lured acclaimed long-distance swimmer, Lynne Cox, on whose behalf I secured an in-kind product sponsorship from Du Pont. In August 1987 she swam between Big and Little Diomede Islands, putting a bit of a thaw in Cold War tensions when her success was praised by both Ronald Reagan and Mikhail Gorbachev. But that was an athletic feat. Schurke's project had serious diplomatic goals in mind.

So here we are in Anadyr, the expedition team of six Soviets and six Americans, sponsors, the indefatigable Jason Davis, and a support crew assembled for the final send-off. Also along for the ride are media representatives we convinced to buy tickets for the flight, reporters from the Associated Press, *National Public Radio, Reuters, San Francisco Examiner, Voice of America,* and Anchorage TV stations and newspapers. Fifty-seven of us on a chartered Alaska Airlines Boeing 737 dubbed "Friendship One." In the cargo hold are one dozen sled dogs and provisions for the long expedition to come. I was feeling pretty confident that coverage for this venture would be a home run.

The flight departs March 1, 1989, and in just two hours travel time across the Bering Strait, it arrives in Anadyr on March 2, about twenty hours later on the calendar. We are literally traveling into tomorrow thanks to the International Date Line, the border between the U.S. and Soviet Union, an imaginary point at 180 degrees longitude, give or take a few diversions, where yesterday meets today.

Our arrival is met by bitter cold—the pilot reports minus fifteen degrees Fahrenheit and thirty mph winds—creating a windchill of minus forty-six degrees Fahrenheit. In these conditions, no matter what you're wearing, it becomes difficult to think. Words slur. It's the kind of cold that hits you in the face like a frozen codfish.

The sickening smell of jet fuel hangs in the air as we land in this godforsaken place, the first commercial U.S. flight to do so since the World War II Lend-Lease program in the 1940s. We are met by a welcoming committee of 100 people who were bearing, of all things, a sculpted loaf of bread on an embroidered towel, with some salt nesting in a hole on top. The bread is offered by two stunningly beautiful women in native dress and represents hospitality; in this part of the world, salt is associated with long friendship. It seems fitting, given the theme of the expedition, although if they really want to impress, a couple of Jon-e Hand Warmers would be a nice touch about now.

I remain busy recording the scene on my Nikkormat camera, dressed in a gaudy bright red expedition parka with large logos depicting the three Du Pont products we were promoting: Thermax, Quallofil, and Thermoloft. I am decked out like a walking billboard, like a polar racecar driver, but I'm dressed this way unapologetically, knowing how visual identification for a sponsor's brand could help generate awareness in news coverage.

We are all celebrities when the Friendship Flight arrives. There are bear hugs, air kisses, and lots of backslapping. The local media swarm around us. Within minutes of deplaning, a Soviet television reporter asks me for first impressions of the Soviet Union. As I turn one of my Du Pont patches ever-so-slightly toward the cameras, I keep my opinions to myself: this is a dreary place of apparently warm, friendly people living otherwise humorless lives in drab cinder-block buildings with 1950s-era appliances. Their bathrooms aren't so great either, as I am soon to learn.

School buses and Jeeps idle nearby to transport us one mile to town. There are police at every intersection as the motorcade passes. Once in the town center, we enter a stuffy cinder-block auditorium and are astonished to find some 300 townspeople gathered in their Sunday finest. The Bering Bridge team walks onto the stage of the Anadyr Cultural Center. The sound system launches into the Russian national anthem, followed by the U.S. national anthem. Tears well up in our eyes. This expedition, which worked so hard to gain permits, recruit both American and Russian team members, secure sponsors, and attract the media, is about to start.

A lunch follows in a local school that features copious amounts of vodka. In fact, vodka is at every place setting, along with pitchers of water, strange fish delicacies, breads of all varieties, caviar, and flags. These people love their flags. The table is decorated with small Soviet and American flags on little plastic stands—and more high-octane Russian vodka. In fact, the ensuing lunch, punctuated by continual cries of "Peace" and the Russian equivalent, "*Mir*," seem lubricated by a flow of what we start to call, after a few glasses, "wod-kuh." I notice, somewhat bleary-eyed, that our newfound Soviet friends are taking great pleasure in their ability to drink their American guests under the table.

My fluency in Russian is growing the more vodka I consume. I thank everyone with a hearty "spa-see-bah," introduce myself with "me-nyah za-voot Jeff," and say good-bye—"doe-svee-dan-i-yeh"—even when I meant to say hello. By now it is the vodka talking, not me.

Paul, in his book, *Bering Bridge: The Soviet-American Expedition from Siberia to Alaska* (Pfeifer-Hamilton, 1989), tells of one Soviet woman, in tears, who tugged at a reporter's jacket and said through an interpreter, "I never thought I would live to see the day when Americans would land in peace in our town."

As for me, I never thought I'd live to see the day I'd visit a bathroom that consisted of just a hole in the ground and two platforms for your feet. The horror was compounded by coarse toilet paper embedded with bits of wood chips, and one dirty cloth that was encrusted to a towel bar next to the sink. I decided I'd wait until I was back on the plane.

About one week later, the team began its crossing of the ice-clogged Bering Strait in a traditional thirty-foot by five-foot Eskimo boat—a umiak—made of walrus skin, based upon a design perfected through thousands of years of trial and error. Two Siberian Yupik seal hunters piloted the explorers through eight-foot swells and poor visibility, using only a compass for navigation.

Paul called the journey "nerve wracking." According to his interview with Sherri McBride, a reporter for the *Nome Nugget*, part of the six-hour voyage was ideal and relatively calm with magnificent scenery, while at other times snow squalls and pockets of fog assailed them. McBride reported, "There were miles of open water where the sea ice broke the waves, or they bobbed on big swells, and one-eighth of an inch of walrus hide and a wood frame were all that separated members of the team from destiny."

Paul would later remember the crossing in his book, *Bering Bridge*: "I was completely out of my element. I considered how relative courage and comfort are. Being tagged an 'adventurer' doesn't exempt one from fear," he writes.

First stop was Soviet-controlled Big Diomede, within sight of the International Date Line. Arriving on the southern shore, the team hiked for miles in the dark as they searched for the border patrol station that was awaiting their arrival. Border guards had built a bonfire, bathed the shoreline in light, shot green flares into the sky, and fired up the lighthouse to help the team find their way. The entire station was aglow as the team arrived to a welcome of whoops and hugs, hot soup, black bread, and tea.

During their three-day visit to Big Diomede, team members played soccer with the Soviet Border Patrol and established radio communications with the Bering Bridge Expedition office in Nome, about 100 miles away.

Meanwhile, I am attempting my own expedition to attend goodwill ceremonies on the Date Line with members of the media and Steve Cowper, then governor of Alaska. It is a nice try. The day is April 23, 1989, and while Jason is in full Edward R. Murrow mode, that morning I find myself stranded in a dreary airport hanger near Nome with the Governor and his entourage, awaiting a National Guard Blackhawk helicopter to whisk us to the ceremony. But the flight never takes off. We are grounded, socked in by fog. This is a grim place in winter, a time when the sun goes down in November, not to be seen again until February. At least the local slogan, "There's no place like Nome," was spot on. Were it not for the Iditarod dogsled race that terminates there each March, you wouldn't hear much about the place.

The experience teaches me the importance of traveling with enough reading material to choke a horse. Reading, and re-reading the *Nome Nugget* all day doesn't so much pass time as it makes time grind to a virtual standstill. The local convention and visitors bureau presents us all with mock "Arctic Express Cards" with a picture of a hairy walrus instead of the famous AMEX centurion, below the motto: "Don't Leave Nome Without It." But alas, we are in a desolate hanger in one of the western-most towns in the U.S. There is no place to shop for anything, no diversions, no iPods, no Netflix movies on a laptop, simply no place to go in the fog that shrouds the countryside like a thick coating of pea soup.

Miles away, out in the middle of a frozen ocean, Jason is completely in his element, in a blizzard no less, the same nasty weather that cancelled our flight. Thanks to a satellite earth dish anchored to the ice, he is about to nail the first-ever live broadcast from the middle of the Bering Strait.

The team is met at the Date Line by more than thirty U.S. and Soviet officials for an emotional ceremony held in appalling weather—thick fog, blowing snow, frigid ten degrees Fahrenheit temperatures, and biting fifteen mph winds. Meanwhile, the governor's welcoming committee is toast. Weathered out of the festivities, we drive back into Nome to huddle around a seven-inch screen to watch the satellite feed. Coverage of the forty-five-minute ceremony is being broadcast live to the Soviet Union and throughout Alaska over the strangely named RATNET—Rural Alaska Television Network.

Once holed up far from the action, I watch the live feed intensely for signs of our Thermax patches that were carefully sewn on the parkas weeks before. The wind is blowing so hard, American and Soviet flags are flying at attention straight out, snapping in the wind. As a yellow Aeroflot Mil Mi-8 helicopter hovers in the background between swirls of blowing snow, I occasionally glimpse Tony Bell, the outdoor adventure photographer we hired for the occasion. Tony was given a container of RIT dye in case he had to actually create a Date Line on the ice. As it was, the border was already clearly surveyed and marked in orange by Alascom, the Alaskan communications company. The Soviets built a green wooden obelisk about six feet tall for the photo opp.

Plenty of photos are taken, team members enjoy a jumbo package of Peanut M&M's and choke as a Soviet film producer inexplicably lights a smoke flare and holds it aloft. Shortly thereafter, a joint U.S.-Soviet statement of intent is signed during a telephone conversation between Governor Cowper and his Soviet counterpart to encourage visa-free travel between the two countries. For us, the biggest hardship is cold coffee. For the team, it is a far different story. They experience cold everything. They had spent the previous fifty days dogsledding and cross-country skiing through snowdrifts as high as twelve feet and temperatures cold enough to freeze boiling water before it hit the ground.

Paul reported winds reaching sixty miles per hour at times and a one-hundred-foot snow ledge that nearly swallowed a whole dog team. It made for great newspaper copy, of course, so long as they didn't freeze to death in their Du Pont Thermax long underwear, socks, glove liners, and hats. Wintergreen Designs of Ely had a special interest in helping the Bering Bridge team survive—much of the team clothing was custom-made by Paul's wife, who also created cold-weather clothing for the 1986 Steger North Pole Expedition.

While the team braved the cold, harsh Arctic conditions, we breathlessly issued press releases that made it appear as if Thermax thermalwear fabric was the true hero of the expedition, because, well, that's what sponsors do. Paul, as cocaptain of the project along with the Russian adventurer Dmitry Shparo, gamely played along: "The goodwill goals of this effort cannot be achieved if frostbite and hypothermia force us to turn back," he said in a company press release. Nonetheless, we knew that if the media ignored our prepared statements, we also had the benefit of strong visual identification on the team outfits, and of course, whatever coverage Jason Davis could throw our way.

Attention of a different sort, the unwanted kind, occurred shortly after the Date Line ceremony, when two Soviet journalists, both Moscow students in their twenties, slinked away from the main group on Little Diomede and approached a member of the Eskimo Scouts, a unit of the Alaska National Guard. Like a scene from a mediocre Robin Williams movie, the two politely inquired whether it would be possible to seek political asylum on this tiny granite patch of American soil.

The dumbfounded scout checked with his commanding officer, then returned to ask if they were serious. They were deadly serious, knowing they risked imprisonment back home, especially since one of the officials on the Soviet welcoming committee was widely known to be a KGB agent.

Paul was livid. In his book about the expedition, he remembers, "I felt ripped off. They had used us. They had taken advantage of our goodwill event for their own gain."

The regional office of the U.S. Immigration and Naturalization Service immediately took over and plans were made to fly the two to Nome, then Anchorage. The Soviet members of the team were mortified. The Governor's office was dismayed that the defection would hamper a number of joint cooperative programs under development for years.

Governor Cowper would remember the incident on that bleak island in the middle of nowhere when I contacted him years later: "If you have ever been to Little Diomede, [the defection] was a pretty unfavorable commentary on conditions in the USSR at the time," he said.

The students had been planning to defect for two years and forged letters from their college newspaper to join Russian reporters covering the team. They would eventually be granted asylum and work papers. There was one silver lining in the incident. Paul later wrote, ". . . the world was reawakened to the cultural bond between Soviet and American Eskimos."

Following the Date Line event, the team was treated to an exhibition of native dancing in the Little Diomede school gymnasium. Another highlight of Little Diomede: a new shipment of long underwear arrived, a welcome respite from wearing the same pairs for fifty days on the trail. "It was time for a change," Paul told the media.

Although the Date Line ceremony and the defection made news around the world, the expedition was hardly over by then. There were still another twenty-two miles of strait to cross before reaching the Alaskan mainland. Unfortunately, it was clogged with more ice than water, making it totally impassable by either umiak or dogsled. An airlift was their only option.

Once the team's dogs, equipment, and supplies were transported by plane to Wales, Alaska, they faced hundreds of additional miles of sledding along the coastline en route to the Alaskan town of Kotzebue, located just above the Arctic Circle, that imaginary line of latitude at sixty-six degrees north that marks the southern point of the midnight sun.

In early May, the expedition concluded with celebratory speeches, songs, and dance performances in Kotzebue. A team that suffered exhaustion and bouts of snow blindness after enduring the region's most severe weather in four decades now had a real challenge ahead—a grueling press tour to Anchorage, Seattle, Minneapolis, Duluth, and New York that would prove to be almost as daunting. For the team, coming back to reality was a cold slap in the face, especially in New York where a rapist was loose in their hotel and a murder occurred in a restaurant only hours after they dined there.

These days, Paul and Susan Schurke continue to run a handcrafted outdoor apparel business called Wintergreen Northern Wear in Ely, and Wintergreen Dogsled Lodge, the county's only resort devoted exclusively to dogsledding, according to *National Geographic Traveler*. *Backpacker* magazine called him the "King of Cool," and in 2002, *Outside magazine* ranked Wintergreen among the "Top Ten" most innovative and influential outdoor companies of the past quarter century and considers Wintergreen's Greenland trips among the "Top 25" adventures of a lifetime.

For about $100,000 in cash sponsorship and another $150,000 in goods and services, the expedition succeeded in "breaking the ice" in an effort to reestablish cultural relations between Soviet and American Eskimos. And thanks to the help of media coverage, sponsors went along for the ride.

An avid winter sports enthusiast all my life, I grew up skiing in the 1950s and can remember rope tows, wooden skis, screw-in edges, lace-up boots, and liftlines that reached a quarter of the way up Holiday Mountain, my tiny local ski hill in the Catskills. I recall waiting eagerly for the latest ski magazines to arrive, promising myself that when I finally entered Syracuse University and an opportunity arose to ski out west, I would be on the next plane. Or something like that. Living on a poor college student's budget meant that first trip to Aspen was a twenty-six-hour car ride—each way—an experience that makes me avoid long distance driving to this day. Four belching, farting, foul-mouthed, testosterone-poisoned ski fanatics in a rented Hertz, each driving one tank of gas per turn, never cutting off the engine except to refuel, eating gas-station hot dogs cooked on little rotating steel rods. It was hard to believe that car could ever be rented again.

I was a ski reporter at Syracuse University, writing about the sport for a local weekly newspaper. In a shameful effort to scam free lift tickets from Central New York ski areas, I was also the ski reporter on the college radio station, hosting a show called *Ski Scene* for four winters.

Once I hit the working world, I transitioned from writing about the sport to promoting ski resorts. I thought I had died and gone to heaven. One of my earliest assignments was for Ski the Rockies, a marketing association of twelve destination resorts in five western states. That was followed by assignments for the Ski the Summit resorts in Summit County, Colorado, and a stint handling public relations for the Killington Ski Resort in Vermont. It didn't seem like work when you had to travel to a ski resort for business. Somehow, I'd figure a way to turn a three-hour meeting into a four-day visit. A "site inspection," I'd call it.

In 1993, I was asked to promote a training run for another one of Will Steger's epic adventures, the International Arctic Project, a six-month, 2,500-mile crossing of the Arctic Ocean from Russia to Canada by dog team and canoe. The training for the big trip would be almost as grueling—a 2½ month, 1,000-mile dogsled trek across Canada's Northwest Territories, from Yellowknife, Northwest Territories, to Churchill, Manitoba. The objective was to strengthen and train both explorers and sled dogs and test specially designed canoes that would allow them to safely cross ice flows and the dangerous open water of the Arctic Ocean two years later.

As before, we knew it would be important to engage the media by hosting them on a memorable Arctic adventure—take them dogsledding, feed them caribou hot dogs, and join Steger and his team as they interacted with local schoolchildren in Yellowknife, the departure point of the training trip.

On the invitation list were freelancers for *American Health, Men's Health, Men's Journal,* and *Outside* magazines, plus the *Wall Street Journal.* Also along was a ski-industry friend, a hard-working freelance writer named Mike Finkel, one of the most creative, most humorous ski writers I know.

Based in Bozeman, Montana, Mike's career has blossomed over the years, beyond skiing, into the mainstream. He has written for the *Atlantic Monthly, National Geographic Adventure, Rolling Stone, Esquire, Sports Illustrated,* and the *New York Times Magazine.* In 2005 he wrote a book called *True Story* about a man wanted for killing his wife and three young children, a charlatan who assumed Mike's identity at a particular low point in his journalism career. But I knew Mike before all of that, when I saw promise in this budding adventure writer starting with his first story in *Ski* magazine about going skiing on spring break with his father. I believed Steger's expedition would receive great exposure if I added Mike to the group of media I was inviting to the Arctic.

Mike and I had this common bond. Skiing was as much a part of his life as my own. "Skiing has ruined my life," he would write in his book, *Alpine Circus* (The Lyons Press, 1999). "My attachment to the sport has dashed any plans I've ever had for a stable or financially secure career. Because of skiing, I have been both ceremoniously and unceremoniously dumped by a lift line's worth of wonderful, marriageable women."

Yellowknife, with a population of about 15,000, is the capital of the Northwest Territories, an area larger than Europe, and one of the world's leading gold-mining towns. It is surrounded by a frozen, desolate region called the Barrenlands, which stretch for hundreds of miles. Interviewing a local with his four-by-eight-inch reporter notebook, of which he has dozens, Mike would later write that the wizened fisherman with a face lined like a topographic map described his homeland as being "so flat you can watch your dog run away for two days." But even dogs are too smart for that; the nearest major city, Edmonton, is a twenty-two-hour drive south.

Upon arrival at our hotel, Mike and I quickly hit town with a few other media guests in tow. Our first stop, the Gold Range, was right out of the bar scene in *Star Wars*. It was the first bar I've ever visited that had a mesh screen in front of the stage to protect musicians from flying beer bottles and pitchers. The natives nicknamed the place the "Strange Range," and I could see why.

After warming up our pitching arms with a few pitchers, we went outside for the real show in town. There, just below the main street, out on an ice highway that stretched for miles across the frozen Great Slave Lake, and vibrated with a sort of rolling motion as every large truck passed by, we were witness to a spectacular nighttime performance of the aurora borealis, a phenomenon also known as the northern lights, usually associated with sunspots, solar flares, and disturbances in both the ionosphere and the earth's magnetic field. Under a night sky illuminated bright enough to read a newspaper, we were treated to shimmering curtains and swirls of light. It was breathtaking.

According to local legend, these shimmering fires that sweep across the polar sky are torches held up by the gods to provide aid for wintertime hunting. Moki Kokoris writes in the *Polar Times*, "... ancient people gazed up at the night skies and saw in them ceremonial journeys of angels, departed ancestors, supernatural creatures, and children yet unborn."

Locals told me you can make the northern lights dance by rubbing fingernails together and whistling. I learned that Norwegians wave white handkerchiefs in the air to make them appear. The Japanese believe that making love under these ethereal displays would result in academically gifted offspring. Tourism officials in Yellowknife do little to dissuade them of the belief. The prevailing attitude was that visitors can do whatever they wanted on their own sweet time, so long as they continued to spend money in local hotels and restaurants.

Mike would write that the experience was "transcendent and spiritual and otherworldly . . . streaks merged, like drops of mercury gathering together, and there appeared a single wall of lambent green light, hanging from the heavens and undulating like a curtain in front of an open window.

"It was a show so dazzling I scarcely moved for almost two hours."

Viewing the northern lights with the media—taking them to share experiences you may encounter no matter where your dream trip takes you—does more to promote an expedition than any press conference, three-martini Manhattan lunch, or email blast could ever hope to achieve.

How To Engage the Media

☞ **Target Editors and Reporters**—Read outdoor adventure magazines voraciously and prepare a target list of media; you can gather names off the masthead or from story bylines. Buy media directories to identify editors and reporters to approach, or better yet, search "outdoor magazines" on Google. Another idea: review magazines and newspapers in the periodical section of your local library, or buy copies of the actual outdoor and adventure publications, which you'll probably want to be reading anyway—one or more of their advertisers could help pay for your trip. Don't forget to identify business-to-business trade magazines as well, particularly in your target sponsor's industry. Planning a pedal boat crossing? Add *Boating Industry, Soundings Trade Only, International Boating Industry News*, and other marine trade magazines and Web sites to your reading list.

☞ **Introduce Yourself**—Send an email, place a quick introductory call, or mail editors, producers, or reporters a note. Yes, just like in the Stone Ages—a real paper envelope, a typed note, and a postage stamp. Keep all communication brief. No one has a lot of time to read long letters or emails. Practice your elevator pitch—what would you say if you had just ten seconds to describe your trip? It's a commercial, not a miniseries.

☞ **Provide a Taste of Adventure**—Consider how the media can experience your project—invite them to the send-off, meet with them during key trip milestones, encourage them to attend arrival ceremonies. Give media a taste of the adventure: a dogsled ride, kayaking on a calm day, mountain biking, or cross-country skiing—whatever activity is relevant to your project.

☞ **Don't Forget To Write**—Suggest that the media opt-in to your email updates so you can keep them posted as the project proceeds. Create an email list of everyone you've ever reached, including friends and relatives, and keep them in the loop.

☞ **Track Results**—Secure all the media coverage you can find to share with sponsors. Friendly reporters may mail you copies of their coverage, you can sign up for Google Alerts to receive them automatically as stories are published, or do it the old-fashioned way—actually go out and buy the magazine or newspaper when your story appears. Television and radio coverage is also available for purchase.

☞ **Stay in Touch**—Once the trip concludes, stay in touch with the media about news of your next project. If they covered you once, they might do so again.

CAN YOU HEAR ME NOW?
TECHNOLOGY'S ROLE IN ADVENTURE MARKETING

STARS AND STRIPES NAILED TO THE NORTH POLE—PEARY.
This long-awaited message from American explorer Robert E. Peary
(1856–1920) flashed around the globe by cable and telegraph the afternoon of September 6, 1909. Reaching the North Pole, a three-century
struggle that had taken many lives, was the equivalent of the first manned
landing on the moon. Achieving this expeditionary Holy Grail was mon-
umental news, except it came about five months late. Peary and his team,
including African-American Matthew A. Henson, are generally recognized to have actually arrived at the "Big Nail," as the North Pole was
called, months before, on April 6.

Communicating news about expeditions wasn't much better in the
mid-to-late sixties when I was attending Monticello Middle School in
the New York Catskills. We had a welcome break from rote classroom
learning when, during the recovery of one of the Mercury space capsules,
the entire school gathered in the auditorium to watch a single black and
white television. Coverage at that time consisted of an image of CBS
News correspondent Dallas Townsend, a slide of the *U.S.S. Enterprise*
recovery vessel, and for some visual interest, a map of the ocean splash-
down site. Townsend used a radiophone to provide a blow-by-blow de-
scription as an astronaut was plucked from the sea. Expedition coverage
gradually became more instantaneous over the following twenty years.
The first live images from the summit of Mount Everest were sent via

microwave transmission on May 7, 1983, by mountaineer and filmmaker David Breashears. Sherpa Ang Rita, who knows the summit of Everest as well as any human alive (he bagged his tenth summit in 1996), pointed the microwave transmitter while Breashears ran the camera for the ABC TV program *American Sportsman.*

"The summit images were transmitted live seventeen miles to the Mount Everest View Hotel where they were recorded on videotape," David would tell me years later. From there the videotape was flown to Kathmandu where the images were uplinked via satellite to New York.

David explains in his book, *High Exposure* (Simon & Schuster Paperbacks, 1999), "We weren't going to try a satellite uplink directly from Everest to the States because, back then, most expeditions made the summit around two or three p.m., which would be two or three a.m. in the U.S. There'd be no one awake to watch that live broadcast."

In a later interview for *Expedition News,* he said, "Imagine the delight and surprise of the video technicians who were the first to see live images from earth's highest point."

As recently as 1986, when Will Steger and his team reached the North Pole without resupply, news traveled by radio to Resolute Bay, about 1,100 miles away, then by telephone and fax to Steger's friends and family in St. Paul. Responsible for promoting his expedition on behalf of Du Pont, my staff and I couldn't leave anything to chance. We needed a point person to communicate news about the expedition to the media. Jennifer Kimball, a bright, energetic account executive at the agency, was tapped to handle the project. Jennifer, who bore a striking resemblance to a young Meryl Streep, always wanted to travel, although a trip to Steger's base station in the small Inuit hamlet of Resolute Bay, one of the coldest inhabited places on earth, was hardly on her bucket list. But ask Jennifer about the assignment today, and a warm smile comes across her face. It was a journey that changed the course of her life.

The story begins in 1986 on the sixty-sixth floor of the Empire State Building, home of Blumenfeld and Associates, which we semi-seriously promoted as New York's tallest public relations agency. Sure, there were larger agencies, but none above the sixty-sixth floor either in the Empire State Building or within its downtown rival, the World Trade Center.

Will Steger was preparing for his Steger North Pole Expedition, an attempt to prove that it would have been possible for Robert E. Peary to travel to the North Pole by dogsled in 1909. In the six decades since Peary's expedition, dirigibles, airplanes, and submarines have journeyed to ninety degrees north latitude. Yet it was only until 1968 that the Pole was reached by surface route. Minnesota insurance salesman Ralph S. Plaisted, supported by fifty companies including Pillsbury and the makers of Knorr dried soups, relied upon sixteen-horsepower Ski-Doo snowmobiles for the feat. When he returned, the St. Paul *Pioneer Press* quoted him, "Boy, it's cold up there. I don't know why anyone would want to do it again."

Undeterred, Steger, an ardent student of history, set his sights on trekking to the Pole the old fashioned way, the Peary way, using sled dogs.

A wiry and resourceful Minnesotan named Jim Gasperini was selected to manage the Steger team logistics from Resolute Bay, working out of a WWII-era Quonset hut—a corrugated galvanized iron building—used by a local carrier named First Air, "The Airline of the North." Jim, a law student studying for his bar exam, was also responsible for relaying information from the team back to its sponsors, to the Blumenfeld agency, friends, and loved ones. While today's explorers can communicate worldwide by satellite and Internet directly from the field, in the mid-1980s relaying messages by high frequency radio to a base camp and then to a hard telephone line was the most reliable method of getting the word out.

Once Jim was linked to the team by radio, he forwarded messages to Jennifer in New York by phone and fax. Jennifer and Jim were in daily contact, soon forming a polar bond that would deepen as the fifty-six-day expedition unfolded. The calls back and forth weren't all business. As the two got to know each other, they started faxing photos back and forth. Jim would send a staid group shot of himself with some local pilots; Jennifer, a particularly playful member of our small staff, would send a photo of a surfing babe from a magazine. Jim grew more curious and flirtatious and suggested that the best way to serve her Du Pont client, the largest sponsor of the expedition, was to come to Resolute herself.

As a single, savvy, twenty-six-year-old woman from New York, Jennifer was wise to superficial and shallow New York men. Her BS meter was always set on high. Who was this slow-talking, laid back guy? Was he coming on to her? Quite possibly, she reasoned, especially considering that Resolute Bay, with its population hovering around 200, lacked companionship of the female variety, and Jim had been alone in the Arctic for many weeks by now. But Jennifer was forging a career in adventure marketing, and a trip to the Arctic seemed like the adventure of a lifetime.

Arriving at Resolute Bay's airport, she met Jim for the first time. He was a little shorter than she expected, but with blue eyes and blond hair, he was far better looking than the usual types you find hanging out at polar weigh stations.

Years later Jennifer would tell Drienie Hattingh, a reporter for the *Woodbury Bulletin,* her local newspaper in Minnesota, that she was mesmerized by the surroundings. It was May and close to midnight, yet the sun was sitting low on the horizon and shining directly into her face. It was so white, so cold, yet in a way, so pure. Snowdrifts lined both sides of the street ten to twelve feet high. Upon arrival, Jim walked her to the Narwhal Hotel, named for a species of whale with one long single tusk— like a unicorn of the sea. Her room was simple, basic, about what you'd expect for accommodations in a Quonset hut. Sleep would be difficult. At that latitude, where the sun shines constantly from April to August, insomnia is to be expected. At midnight, when it looks like noon, you have to make a conscious effort to fall asleep. There are no visual cues. A sleep mask, blackout curtains, and some thick covers over your head are your only hope.

Jim and Jennifer soon began to work together as a team. It was mostly all business—Jennifer would bang out expedition updates on her portable typewriter, then fax them to New York. Jim, meanwhile, was in regular radio contact with the team as they neared the Pole. During quiet moments, Jim would make lunch, talk about studying law, his love of children, and share with Jennifer common interests in movies, music, and far away places. She started thinking this bearded, low-key guy was different from anyone else she'd met in New York, someone who offered "everything she could have wanted in a man," as she later admitted to the *Woodbury Bulletin.*

As the team neared the North Pole, everyone was stressed. The media were making demands on the two—every reporter wanted to land a first interview with the Steger team—yet radio communications were spotty, and tempers were running high. Jim needed a break and suggested that Jennifer join him for a walk to a three-story iceberg that had floated into a nearby bay. They set off for two hours—Jennifer, this woman from New York who grew up in the safe, if rather boring suburb of Darien, Connecticut, and Jim, her polar buddy, dressed in beaver gloves, fur hood, frosted beard, and rifle over his shoulder. "For protection against polar bears," he would tell her.

She told the *Woodbury Bulletin,* "It seemed so unreal, as if it was a scene out of a movie. Just the two of us in the frozen landscape, dressed in all the Arctic gear, and him with a gun—my protector." To this day, she considers that walk their first date together.

They returned to base not long before the team reached the Pole. Shortly afterward, Jim left for the twenty-four-hour roundtrip flight to pick up the team and the sled dogs. Jennifer found herself missing him. Her heart skipped a beat when he called in by radio to say hello.

She was developing a crush on the guy and looked for signs that he felt the same way. He did. On the plane home he saved a seat for her, then didn't flinch when she rested her head on his shoulder. Back in St. Paul, he introduced Jennifer to his family in that special manner sons use to indicate that this isn't just any girlfriend. This one might be a keeper.

The two maintained a long-distance relationship just like in the old days, which the mid-1980s certainly were when you consider the lack of cell phones, email, Web cams, Facebook, or Twitter. Jim's gain was my loss, as one year later Jennifer resigned from the agency, packed her bags, and moved to Minnesota. He proposed during a winter cross-country outing in Lake Tahoe. A romantic storybook wedding followed that summer at her family's church in New England. Today Jennifer and Jim have three children: Ellesha, Tucker, and a particularly adventurous and inventive youngest son named Will, in honor of the famed polar explorer who brought them together.

While Jennifer and Jim were rubbing noses like Eskimoses, we were busy with the "Call of the Wild" Polar Phone—a call-in number that was updated weekly. It provided a thirty-second report on the team's progress, then ended with a shameless plug for survival gear insulated with Du Pont fibers. Recorded by professional radio announcer Morrie Trumble, a well-known radio and television ski reporter, it logged thousands of calls over the course of the expedition despite the fact that it was a toll call for anyone outside of New York.

Through these efforts, the Steger North Pole Expedition caught the public's fancy. Paul Schurke, a coleader of the effort, would later tell Robert Sullivan of *Sports Illustrated*, "I figured it would interest the folks in Minnesota because it highlighted a lot of things we're proud of here: the frontier spirit, little people doing something big, winter exploring, and adventuring in general. Lindbergh's still our biggest local hero. I was stunned that the whole nation tuned in like it did."

A few years later, the Polar Phone was back, this time in support of the 1989–90 Trans-Antarctica Expedition. The tollfree number provided weekly one-minute status reports. Radio stations played the message on-air. Children took turns calling and reporting back to their classes. By the end of the expedition, 192,000 calls had been logged at a cost of about $32,000 in telephone charges. The effort was considered a great success in those days before the Web became commonplace.

Minnesota explorer Dan Buettner was another early pioneer in using technology to link his expedition directly to home- and school-based audiences. In 1995, his MayaQuest, an interactive expedition through Central America, used laptop computers and satellite equipment to enable online users to direct—and contribute to—Dan's scientific expedition in real time.

To study why the ancient Mayan civilization collapsed in the ninth century AD, the 105-day expedition traveled 3,224-miles through the Yucatan Peninsula, filing reports from Dzibilchaltun, Chichen Itza, Nakbe, and Okulwitz. The expedition stumbled onto an unrecorded site in southern Mexico. It also found a crystallized skull, ancient footprints, and 1,300-year-old pots a mile deep in a Belize cave—all great fodder for stimulating young minds addled by too much TV. Through this early use of the Internet, Dan harnessed the collective wisdom of thousands of schoolchildren to consider causes of the Mayan Collapse—a "Perfect Storm" of environmental degradation, growing disparity between rich and poor, and an extended drought. Kids followed along online, at times asking the team questions and even helping plan its agenda, linked to the field through a portable router, an Ethernet hub, a twelve-volt battery, two Apple PowerBook 5300cs laptops, a collapsible $33,000 Rockwell satellite dish the size of a small kitchen table, and a snarl of wires.

~~~

Today explorers need more than just a good concept, sufficient funding, and proper training. Technology has raised the bar, requiring sophisticated knowledge of new communications equipment made possible by satellites, durable rechargeable batteries, solar panels, and the Internet. Sponsors, educators, and the media alike expect to follow an expedition each day from the comfort of their laptops. Tell a schoolchild today you once had to assemble in an auditorium to watch NASA space coverage on a single black and white television, and they will assume it was so long ago dinosaurs were probably still roaming the earth.

In this age of instant gratification, kids want to talk to explorers *right now* and follow along in real time. This need for instant communications—combined with the alarming growth of childhood obesity—is what drove Denver schoolteacher Mike Haugen.

Mike and executives at Coleman, the over-100-year-old manufacturer of camping stoves, lanterns, and picnic coolers, became alarmed at statistics pointing to the high incidence of childhood obesity.

It would be one thing if kids were getting enough exercise at school, but that's not the case. The percentage of children ages six to eleven who are overweight has more than doubled in the past twenty years, and the percentage of teens who are overweight has more than tripled during the same period. It is estimated that 15 percent of six- to nineteen-year-olds and more than 10 percent of children two to five years old are obese, according to a University of Michigan review on Physical Education in America's public schools. This is likely due to poor nutrition and low levels of physical activity. Spending an estimated forty-four hours per week hooked to some electronic device such as an iPod or video game doesn't help.

"Nature deficit disorder" is a contributing factor, believes Richard Louv in his book, *Last Child in the Woods: Saving Our Children From Nature Deficit Disorder* (Algonquin Books, 2005). Louv says competition from television and computers, more homework, and other time pressures, plus lack of access to natural areas is keeping kids indoors.

Fear plays a large part in this—fear of traffic, crime, "stranger-danger," and nature itself, according to Louv, who quotes a fourth-grader: "I like to play indoors better 'cause that's where all the electrical outlets are."

Adds Louv, "Never before in history have children been so plugged in—and so out of touch with the natural world."

Coleman reasoned that if kids weren't enjoying the outdoors, then it was unlikely they would grow up to become enthusiastic consumers of the company's outdoor products.

A plan was hatched to sponsor Mike, already an ambassador for the company, on an expedition to Everest. I was brought in, and at the first meeting I reminded them of the "So what?" rule. Clearly, by 2007, Everest had been climbed every which way. First woman, first American woman, first Canadian woman, oldest woman, and so on. It was going to be an expedition to Ho-Hum unless we could come up with a unique hook, something Mike could do differently from other Everest expeditions.

While it wasn't necessarily a new idea, we hired an educational Web development company in Virginia called PE Central to develop a Web site that would allow kids to play an online game based upon how much exercise they performed outdoors. Exercise for sixty minutes or walk

10,000 steps (as measured by a pedometer), and they could progress from one local village on a virtual Everest trek to the next, all the way to the summit of the 29,035-foot mountain.

As a schoolteacher and a climber, Mike, thirty years old, was ideal. For someone so young, he already had an impressive adventure resume—an avid skier, sailor, and mountaineer, he had traveled to over thirty countries and was certified in wilderness medicine, avalanche rescue, and other survival skills.

Standing six feet, five inches, this fit adventurer was all sinew and bone: a lean, mean climbing machine with a nasty scar on his left forearm caused by a climbing rope that wrapped around his forearm, burning it severely.

Starting with a slight geographic handicap—an upbringing in relatively pancake-flat Minnesota, Wisconsin, and Ohio—he decided at the age of sixteen to take a rock-climbing class with Himalayan climber and Everest veteran Andy Politz, who later gained recognition as a member of the 1999 expedition that discovered the body of George Mallory. Mike made his own climbing apparel, pinched pennies, and learned rigging on a ninety-eight-foot replica of Columbus' *Santa Maria* berthed in Ohio.

After receiving his master's degree from Ohio State in evolutionary physiology, in 2003 Mike began guiding for Rainier Mountaineering, Inc. At the time it was the only guide service permitted to operate on Washington's 14,411-foot Mount Rainier, which Mike had already climbed four times. That year he also joined the staff of an inner-city Denver middle school as an eighth-grade science teacher.

The Coleman Everest 5.5 Challenge in 2007 called for Mike to climb Everest and blog about it daily, sending both video and still images back to Coleman using $6,000 worth of laptops, a Thuraya satellite phone, two hand-held HP PDAs, several solar-energy panels, a GPS, two video cameras, and a digital camera.

In March of that year, just a few days before his departure, we organized an inspiring send-off in the schoolyard of Denver's Kepner Middle School. Easier said than done—between the Denver Public Schools and the corporate lawyers at Coleman, we kept faxes humming with insurance liability policies, photo and video releases, and parental permission forms. In fact, we had a seventeen-point checklist of logistics that needed to be addressed in order to ensure a successful event. The signature attraction was a twenty-four-foot climbing wall that provided visual interest for the three local TV crews and two newspapers that interviewed Mike and his students who would follow along online. To promote Coleman's involvement, we displayed company banners, dressed spokespeople in Coleman-imprinted outerwear, and asked a company representative to say a few words.

Mike and his climbing partner, Casey Grom, thirty-two, a full-time Rainier guide, began their Everest attempt two months later after enduring weeks of sheer boredom waiting for the weather to break at the mountain's 17,500-foot base camp. They guided a trip to nearby Island Peak, climbed rotations up and down to Camps II and III to acclimatize, even played Wiffle ball and poker to pass the time.

They could have done even more had they not been fine upstanding young men. Climber and journalist Michael Kodas, author of *High Crimes: The Fate of Everest in an Age of Greed* (Hyperion, 2008) writes about what he calls a "mining-camp mentality" at Everest base camp. Korda tells of drugs and prostitution, con men selling faulty oxygen tanks, and climbers stealing rather than buying their supplies. He says hardcore pornography and centerfolds on tent walls made base camp hostile to women team members, although Mike and Casey saw no evidence of such depravity.

The time had finally come for Mike and Casey to pack up and head skyward. After a few nights at various high-altitude camps along the mountain's south side, they left for the summit at 10:30 p.m. on the evening of May 20, 2007. Mike blogged to the thousands following along online:

> After about an hour of climbing, we caught up to a group that was going much slower than us. We stayed behind them for about an hour until we decided to pass. The snow was deep, and it was tough, but we got to the front of the line. There was a spectacular lightning display in the low clouds off in the distance. The first break we took was at an area called the Balcony at 27,500 feet. We were feeling great at this point, so we only took a ten-minute break and continued on up the mountain.
>
> After the Balcony it gets much steeper, with more rocks, which makes the climbing harder. This section seemed to go on forever, since it just keeps going up and up and up. My feet started getting pretty cold because the climbing was slow and the air kept getting thinner. Finally we got to a relatively flat spot that looked like the summit, but it was actually the south summit at 28,700 feet. This part of the mountain was the most interesting and the best climbing. The south summit turns into a sharp ridge with a 10,000-foot fall on either side.
>
> After navigating the ridge, we came to the most famous part of the climb, the Hillary Step. This is a vertical forty-foot section of rock that leads to the final ridge to the summit. As we were walking along this ridge, the sun was coming up, so we had an amazing view into Nepal and Tibet. After a quick six hours and twenty minutes of climbing from the South Col, we were standing on top of the world. We couldn't have asked for a better day to be standing on top of Mount Everest. The sun was shining, and there was very little wind. We stood on top for over thirty minutes and soaked in our accomplishment.

The descent from the summit was not very interesting. Everything went very smoothly, and we were back in our tent, resting within two and a half hours of leaving the summit. Our plan was to rest for an hour, eat some food, drink some water, and try to make it to base camp within the day.

Then the real drama began. On his descent, Haugen and his teammates helped an unidentified critically injured climber from another team, who had been abandoned at the 27,500-foot Balcony, the only level ground between Camp IV and the summit. "Her team was nowhere to be found, and I'm not sure I could live with myself if we hadn't tried to save her," he told a Columbus, Ohio, newspaper a few weeks later.

Mike's blog account of the rescue is chilling:

Within the first twenty minutes of our rest time, we started getting radio calls that there was a woman on the triangular face of Everest (27,000 feet) who was having a very difficult time. A call went out to International Mountain Guides' (IMG) Dave Hahn to watch for her on his way down. By the time Dave got to her, she was in very bad shape and was nearly unconscious. At this point we all began playing detective trying to figure out what team she was with and where their camp was. We figured out she was with the Nepali Democratic team, and the rest of her teammates were high on the mountain.

Dave had radio communication with some doctors at base camp via Mark Tucker (IMG expedition leader), via me. The doctors advised Dave to inject the patient, named Usha, with a drug called Dexamethasone to help with the effects of cerebral edema. Cerebral edema is where the brain begins to fill up with fluids, which can be a side effect of being at altitude. After Dave gave her the 'Dex,' he had to get her down to lower altitudes or she would surely die. With the help of Lhakpe Rita Sherpa and a few other people, they did an amazing job getting Usha down to the South Col where luckily there was a team of doctors with the Extreme Everest Expedition waiting to help.

Usha was diagnosed with cerebral edema, frostbitten hands, and hypothermia (her body temperature was too low). The doctors said that if she did not get down to lower altitudes with more definitive care, she would die. Since Casey, Dave Hahn, and I are guides and were also headed down that day, we were put in charge of coordinating the rescue. Luckily the Extreme Everest group had a couple of Sherpas and a doctor they could send down with us. Since most people at the South Col had climbed Everest that day and were tired, we only managed to find one more Sherpa from the Asian Trekking Expedition group that would help us.

For the extremely steep and rugged descent down from the South Col, Usha was packaged up in a sleeping bag strapped to a sled. Since carrying her down this terrain would be impossible, we would have to drag her and lower her with ropes. This is a pretty standard rescue procedure, where the patient is actually pretty comfortable and snug with a lot of padding. There was actually a pretty big crew that helped us out of the South Col to the Geneva spur where the steep stuff started. We began rigging lowering systems with a couple of people lowering and a few guiding the sled. The very hard parts were the traverses where we not only had to lower and pull, we had to make sure that Usha and the sled did not roll over. Eventually we figured out a good system that was not quite as fatiguing as when we first started.

We worked our way across the steep Lhotse Face and down through a rocky area called the Yellow Band. Once we got through this area, it got a little easier because we were straight above Camp III, so we did more lowering than guiding the sled, but we were also getting very tired. Before we got to Camp III, the sun had set, and it was starting to get cold. We kept lowering and lowering and finally, just above Camp III, a group of doctors from the Extreme Everest Expedition came up and helped us the rest of the way into camp.

Once we were in Camp III, we handed Usha over to a group of physicians who put her in a tent under medical care. We were confident that she was being given top notch care. By the time we descended the Lhotse face, we had been climbing or rescuing for well over 24 hours, so we were exhausted. A group of IMG Sherpas came to meet us on the glacier to bring us some water and to help us with our packs. As mountain guides, we never let anyone carry our packs, but we were very tired. After a little fake resistance, we gladly gave up our packs, and Dave, Casey, and I stumbled back to Camp II. After two bites of fried rice and a cup of tea, we crawled into our Coleman Exponent tent and went to sleep. Long day.

Casey Grom would later tell an Ohio reporter, "Climbing is like a religion. It's helped us through a lot of difficult times in our lives. This happened to be a time we were able to help someone else."

In the early twentieth century, an account of a daring rescue on Mount Everest would have taken months to tell. Now thousands, including an audience of schoolchildren doting on the team's every word, can quickly learn a lesson that the best-laid plans often go astray.

No sooner had Mike returned than we had a real challenge on our hands for 2008: how were we going to top an Everest climb? What do you do when you've summited the world's tallest peak and are well on your way to completing the Seven Summits? The answer soon became clear to me, but it took some selling to convince Coleman to go along. The idea was far more difficult, far more logistically complicated, and far more costly than an Everest expedition, despite the fact that he'd never have to leave the U.S.

We would have Mike summit the tallest peak in every state and do so in record time. For a group of dedicated climbers and hikers, America's so-called highpoints are cherished locations on the map, and no one knows them better than the 2,850 members of the Highpointers Club based in Golden, Colorado.

These passionate peak baggers hold conventions, print newsletters, sell T-shirts and guide books, and even host a hardy subgroup determined to reach the highpoints of the country's 3,141 counties (called, quite naturally, county highpointing). Not surprisingly, the quirky organization also honors low pointing and tri-pointing (reaching the thirty-four land-based points where three states intersect).

If the words "get a life" immediately come to mind, you don't know Jakk. The club traces its beginning to Jack "Jakk" Longacre of Arcadia, Missouri. His real first name was Jack, but the "c" key was broken on his typewriter, and instead of getting it repaired, he just changed his name in club correspondence. The "Jakk" nickname stuck.

As the story goes, Jack became interested in bagging highpoints after reading entries in summit register books. He purchased a small advertisement in *Outside* magazine that led to thirty inquiries from others similarly infected with summit fever. When additional publicity generated more inquiries, Jack decided to get organized.

By the end of 2008, some 178 people had summited all fifty state highpoints, making them eligible to purchase an engraved hardwood plaque commemorating their efforts. Others can buy an embroidered patch for five states or enameled pins for summiting the highest point in twenty-five, thirty, forty, or forty-eight contiguous states (of which there were only 336 completers by December 2008).

From mountains to molehills, the club doesn't care how its members reach the peaks in each state. In fact, sixteen "drive-up" highpoints can be reached by car. These include the Delaware highpoint (448 feet) in Wilmington, located next to a housing development, and puny Britton Hill (345 feet), the highpoint of Florida, situated just twenty feet from a parking lot near Florala, Alabama.

Jack passed away and went to that really tall highpoint in the sky in 2002, just shy of his sixty-fifth birthday. As a fitting tribute, 700 volunteer highpointers spread his ashes on every HP in the union. But for a group whose motto is "Keep Klimbin'" (back to that broken typewriter again), that wasn't enough. By the time Jack's ashes were fertilizing all fifty state highpoints, members began a quest to "escort Jack" to the highpoints of other countries. And so it began. Now his ashes lie on many international highpoints, representing twenty-five different countries, as well as the North and South Poles, all of the Shires of Great Britain, and the provinces of Austria. Everest was the last of the Seven Summits to be climbed by a Jack-carrying highpointer.

Now if you plan to climb an interesting peak, the Highpointers Club may send you a small packet of his ashes, a "Jack in the Pack" (in reality, just a Ziploc bag), in return for a short trip report and photo. Tell them you know Jack.

Knowing about this avid, if somewhat eccentric group of hikers, we immediately got to work on the Coleman project, calling it the "50 States in 50 Days Adventure." Mike selected his climbing partner—a Seattle architect named Zach Price, age thirty—and corralled his twenty-four-year-old girlfriend Lindsay Danner, of Denver, to serve as driver. We had plenty of camping gear, thanks to Coleman, but needed some wheels for the 24,000-mile journey, of which 15,000 would be driving. Mike and I worked feverishly to convince a range of automotive companies and rental car firms to loan us a car. Finally, in a desperate effort, I sent a blind email to every marketing contact I could find at Toyota, since we had our eyes on a gas-and-electric Highlander Hybrid SUV. I started with the names on company press releases, hoping one or two would stick. It worked. Within hours, I heard back from Toyota's public relations department, and shortly afterward, we had our SUV. Lesson learned: if you don't know whom to contact at a company, send a short email to everyone and hope for the best.

The clock started on June 9, 2008, when Mike and Zach reached the 20,320-foot summit of Alaska's Mount McKinley, a relatively free-standing mountain also known by its original Indian name, Denali, located 150 miles north of Anchorage. The two raced down and quickly flew to Florida to meet Lindsay, climbed aboard the SUV, and began knocking off Eastern seaboard highpoints one by one, often two to three per day.

I was ready for them as they prepared to bag Connecticut's particularly pathetic highpoint—located at 2,380 feet on the southern slope of a mountain whose peak lies in Massachusetts. Knowing they would be eating in dozens of chain restaurants and greasy spoons across this fine land of ours, I wanted to treat them to the Sugar Bowl, a local institution in Darien, Connecticut. Mike, Zach, Lindsay, and a documentary filmmaker tagging along with an HD camera glued to his eye, ate as if it were their last meal. Eggs piled high, slabs of bacon, toast, the works. It was a veritable coronary on a plate that would have stopped the heart of mere mortals. But the team needed their fuel.

"You can't run a bulldozer on a pint of diesel," Mike joked in mid bite.

A quick photo opp with the restaurant owner, who gave the team Sugar Bowl T-shirts, and they were on their way again.

The team's quest in the Northeast passed uneventfully. The lower, flatter peaks were coined "flip flop" highpoints, because it didn't take much to summit them: just park the car and pose in sandals by a sign. Even though some highpoints weren't very difficult to scale, Mike still enjoyed the uniqueness of each one. "Each highpoint has had a special beauty that usually leaves us speechless on the way back to the car," he blogged.

In Stowe, Vermont, we secured a free ride on the resort's gondola so they could quickly summit Mount Mansfield.

New Hampshire's Mount Washington was a piece of cake, thanks to an eight-mile auto road that thousands drive to the summit each year. Mike and company were greeted by rains and high wind, but nothing like that day in 1934 when weather observers recorded the earth's highest surface wind speed—231 mph—while hunkering down in a wood-frame building still shackled with heavy chains to prevent it from literally blowing off the mountain.

I've been there in winter, staying overnight in the 6,288-foot summit's fortresslike bunker during a project for Duofold apparel. The summit shelter is built so solidly, the concrete so thick, the only audible indication I could detect of near hurricane-force winds howling outside was the ever-so-slight clanging of an exhaust vent over the kitchen stove.

Flatlanders are warned about "Driver's Collapse" on Mount Washington. Since the air on the summit delivers 18 percent less oxygen than at sea level, out-of-shape summer visitors who drive up the access road sometimes keel over with fainting spells at the top of the parking lot stairway. Considering that the top of Mount Washington was just 1,000 feet higher than Mike's home in Denver, the impact on his lungs was minimal.

The 50 States in 50 Days Adventure became more interesting the further west they traveled. Mike and Zach were threatened by a bear on

Idaho's Borah Peak, hiked with a Girl Scout troop on Oklahoma's summit, were pelted by hail on California's Mount Whitney, and ran for their lives to avoid turning "crispy" from nearby lightning strikes on Arizona's Humphreys Peak. In North Dakota, the U-Haul they were hauling developed a flat, delaying them for hours until a mechanic arrived.

Meanwhile, the public followed the project in real-time thanks to a SPOT Satellite GPS Messenger that pinpointed their exact location every ten minutes. Unlike a GPS for the car, the battery-operated SPOT just sits there silently. It won't tell you where you are, but press the rubber "OK" button, and it will send a satellite message to the cell phones and email addresses of friends and loved ones that you're doing fine. Hold down the recessed "911" button, and they'll send out the cavalry. An alert is sent instantly and silently to GEOS Alliance, an international emergency response center that will dispatch local rescue authorities to the SPOT user's exact location. Cry wolf, and it could get very expensive.

We would rely upon the SPOT device constantly to tell us where Mike was located to within twenty-one feet. At one point, Jeanne Wiggin, my high-strung assistant on the project, panicked. She had an interview scheduled in Seattle before the team's Mount Rainier climb, but Mike had been out of cell phone range for hours. While Jeanne knew exactly where Mike and his team were located thanks to SPOT's interface with Google Earth, she couldn't reach them. Jeanne even called the local Ashford, Washington, police to see if they could pull him over, but the authorities apologized that tracking down a wayward peak bagger late for a media appointment wasn't exactly a good use of law enforcement resources. But it was worth a try. Mike would later resurface when he came within range of a cell tower.

At 11:55 a.m. local time on Friday, July 25, 2008, Mike and Zach reached the top of the adventure's fiftieth state highpoint, 13,796-foot Mauna Kea in Hawaii. In so doing, they established a new record for the fastest ascent of America's highpoints with a time of forty-five days, nineteen hours, and two minutes. The previous highpoint record was set in 2005 by Ben Jones of Lynnwood, Washington, with a time of fifty days, seven hours, and 5 minutes, according to the records maintained by the Highpointers Club. Mike and the team would have done even better had they not sandbagged for a few days in Seattle to avoid an expensive ticket change for their Hawaiian flight. "Besides, this wasn't about breaking a record. This was about getting kids outdoors more," Mike remembers. No stranger to extreme climates, for Mike and his team it felt good to chill for a week of R and R in the sunny Aloha State.

Tech Gear to Consider for Your Adventure

☞ **Get Connected**—Polar explorer Ben Saunders of London goes to extremes to save weight on his expeditions. He cuts the labels off his parkas, removes metal tabs from zipper pulls, and goes so far as to cut the handle on his toothbrush which, to start with, is a child's size. Yet, he won't scrimp on communications gear. "The Internet is simply the best medium for sharing an expedition with audiences because they can interact in real time," he told budding explorers at a Royal Geographical Society conference in 2008. "Learning the language of blogs and streaming video is as important today as learning how to use a compass was for early explorers."

Sure, you can go to Best Buy and fumble around, or you can rely on the gear that experienced adventurers and explorers use, bundled especially for high altitude, North Pole, South Pole, and ocean use by New York–based HumanEdgeTech.com. Their ultra-light ready-to-go communication package for Himalayan expeditions, for instance, includes satellite phone, airtime, camera, PDA, all cables, all installations, and CONTACT 4.0 software that tracks the expedition in real time on a Web-based map, and makes it easy to post text and video. It's all packed into a sturdy yellow Pelican case for about $3,900 (humanedgetech.com).

☞ **Passive Avalanche Rescue Systems**—Searching for someone buried in an avalanche is similar to looking for a needle in a haystack, and traditional methods used by rescue teams are slow and labor intensive. You can even up the odds slightly with RECCO reflectors—pinky-size tabs built into popular outdoor apparel, ski and snowboard boots, and helmets that return harmonic radar signals emitted by a special detector used by search and rescue crews. An estimated 20 million reflectors are now available in wearable products produced by more than 200 manufacturers, including Arc'teryx, Atomic Ski Boots, Helly Hansen, The North Face, PRO-TEC Helmets, and Volcom.

The company claims that once on the scene, in a 100-meter by 100-meter avalanche field, it can take twenty rescuers six to twenty hours with long probe poles to search the 10,000-square-meter area. A single rescuer equipped with the RECCO system can take a quick ten to twelve minutes to locate victims. However, experts warn against feeling a false sense of security with such rescue technology. Jill Fredston, one of the country's most experienced authorities on avalanche safety, says, "While it is critical to travel with the necessary rescue gear, be aware that it can contribute to accidents by making us feel safer. If we have the attitude that we'll be okay if something goes wrong, then we are more likely to act in ways that increase the likelihood of something going wrong."

She continues, "The most effective means of staying alive in avalanche country is to learn how not to get caught in the first place" (recco.com).

To become better educated about avalanches and how to avoid them, refer to the organizations listed in the Appendix.

NOW WHAT?

WHEN THINGS DON'T GO ACCORDING TO PLAN

YOU CAN PLAN ALL YOU WANT. TRAIN FOR DAYS DRAGGING HEAVY TRUCK tires along gravel roads. Take classes in alpine-rescue procedures, wilderness first aid, and avalanche safety. But the adventures and expeditions in this book are often dangerous, certainly unpredictable, and subject to the vagaries of wind, cold, Third World transportation systems, and a myriad of other factors that could doom any project to failure. Sled dogs die, team members drop out, a climbing error causes heartbreaking fatalities. I know, I've seen tragedies happen.

The Final Breath

It's almost unthinkable. How could a human take a single breath of air, descend more than 500 feet under water on a weighted sled, and then return to the surface unharmed? Audrey Mestre of France accomplished this feat many times, until it killed her before my eyes in 2002 in the Dominican Republic. The sport of freediving would never be the same. Neither would I.

It wasn't supposed to happen that way. Audrey, then twenty-eight, a marine biology student, was a sponsored athlete of my client, Mares, the Italian dive-equipment company. I was responsible for generating media coverage for her latest dive. Audrey was attempting to officially break the world record with a freedive of 557.7 feet (170 meters), a depth she achieved unofficially during practice dives three days before her death. It was deeper than any freediver had ever descended.

Freediving is considered the oldest method of undersea exploration. Using little more than fins and sometimes a mask, a diver descends on a single breath of air. To many, the sport of breath-hold or apnea diving is the purest form of underwater achievement.

Unlike scuba divers, freedivers are not hindered by the need to ascend slowly to decompress because they have not breathed any air while underwater. Small consolation for a sport that subjects divers to 241 pounds of pressure per square inch, about sixteen times normal atmospheric pressure—akin to having an NFL linebacker standing on every single square inch of your body.

Earlier in the year we toured New York newspaper and magazine offices to promote Audrey's freediving achievements in hopes of generating awareness for the Mares fins she uses during her dives.

We were an odd sight on the streets of midtown Manhattan. There was me, the poorly dressed publicist in too short pants; Audrey, the beautiful, lithe French athlete with the physique of a ballet dancer; and Francisco "Pipin" Ferraras, then forty, Audrey's husband and headstrong trainer. Pipin (pronounced *pih-peen*) is a mercurial Henry Higgins with a Cuban accent, a large, bulky Vesuvius of a man with a bronze shaved head and volcanic temper who could hold his breath for over seven minutes in a swimming pool. Audrey met Pipin during a dive event in Cabo San Lucas while conducting research for her thesis. After an intense romance that started almost on the day they met, they married in 1999. Pipin held the 531.5-feet (162 meters) record for diving without any breathing appliance. That is one hefty set of lungs. But Audrey planned to prove her lungs were even stronger.

On the day of Audrey's attempted record dive, we are on the beach at the Viva Dominicus resort near Bayahibe, Dominican Republic, boarding small skiffs to transfer to the dive boat, a large sailing catamaran 2½ miles off the D.R.'s southeast coast. Departure is delayed by angry storm clouds and torrential downpours, and by midmorning, it is still dark and overcast. I ride out with Audrey and a group of others, excited to tell her about my own scuba dive two days before, only my sixth since becoming certified, this one to a popular local dive location called Anguilla reef.

I am thrilled to be sharing a ride with Audrey, feeling good about becoming a scuba diver myself, and pleased that Audrey is wearing a bright yellow wetsuit with plenty of sponsor logos on it (which would pretty much guarantee visual identification for the Mares brand). I am ready to see Audrey break the world record.

Audrey was a champion in the No Limits category, the most extreme form of the sport, which involves riding a weighted sled down the length of a vinyl-coated stainless steel cable. Forty media people circle the boat like sea-going paparazzi as the sled hangs suspended off the cat's thick boom.

The plan is set. Audrey is to hyperventilate like a Hoover, breathe hard in and out for several minutes, take one deep breath, pull the sled release cord, and rocket to the bottom. Safety divers wearing traditional scuba gear are in place to monitor her descent and ascent along the thin cable at periodic intervals. At the bottom, a safety diver stands by, breathing a special Trimix mixture—oxygen, helium, and nitrogen—used for depths starting at about 100 feet. Once she reaches the record depth, she will inflate a lift bag and race to the surface in a cloud of bubbles, shattering her husband's world record by just over twenty-five feet and becoming the deepest freediver in history.

The sled release mechanism sticks.

Pipin, dressed in a black wetsuit with a Mares logo across the front, wearing a black face mask, yanks it free after a few tries, and Audrey heads down feet first as planned, firmly grasping the crossbar of the sled. On her back is a time data recorder (TDR)—sort of a diver's black box that measures depth and the rate of descent and ascent.

The feat should have taken just over three minutes. In fact, just the day before, she reached that depth in record time, though no judges were present. Today, October 12, 2002, would be different.

A member of her team shouts out the elapsed time in Spanish.

Suddenly, the boom shudders and it becomes apparent that something is terribly, horribly wrong.

Three minutes pass. Nothing. The lift bag bobs to the surface without Audrey, "like a riderless horse, loping home on instinct," Pipin would later remember in his book, *The Dive* (ReganBooks, 2004).

Three thirty. Four minutes.

At around five minutes, Pipin yells out an obscenity, calls for a diving vest, and descends to rescue his wife.

Six minutes pass. At this point she is either breathing from a safety diver's emergency air tank or she has drowned.

At eight minutes thirty-eight seconds Audrey emerges, unconscious, with a faint pulse. There's pink bloody foam coming out of her mouth. We are almost three miles offshore, about an hour from the nearest hospital.

They race Audrey back to shore in the only boat available, a seventeen-foot dinghy with a single outboard engine.

After hitching a ride in, I discover that Audrey is being treated in the Viva Dominicus resort infirmary. Except that the infirmary, if you can call it that, is actually closed. It's being painted, which means Audrey's rescue team is covered in white paint as they continue chest compressions, administer oxygen, and arrange to transfer her to the nearest hospital thirty minutes away in La Romana.

A group of us speed off for the hospital, not far behind Audrey. I don't speak Spanish, but I know a few words. When an orderly whispers "*muerta*" shortly after we arrive, I know this vibrant, beautiful young woman—a top athlete in perhaps one of the world's most dangerous sports—is dead. Pipin would later write, "Her heart, the heart of a lion, had stopped beating."

For weeks leading up to the accident, I was trying to get the media interested in the Audrey Mestre story. I emailed media alerts, sent two or three dozen faxes, and placed numerous long-distance phone calls to media news bureaus based in the Caribbean. It was tough getting the attention of sports writers, who yawned at my pitch. Freediving was a fringe sport. No balls, no bats, no fast cars or horses. Just one woman diving over 500 feet on a single breath of air.

After her death, however, it was a different story. The media started to call me, tracking me down in my hotel room at the Viva Dominicus. I was reminded of the Kirk Douglas character in *Ace in the Hole*.

"Bad news sells best," he told the film's cub reporter, "because good news is no news."

The death of one of America's top freedivers was a tragedy for which none of us signed up. I knew immediately we had to issue a statement. But to get Pipin to focus on this made me feel particularly insensitive to his grief, which he seemed to be handling, at least from the outside, rather stoically. That afternoon we released a simple statement to the media that explained that the cause of death was unknown. Later, in one of the great understatements of all time, the local coroner would determine that her death was due to "drowning."

Questions surrounding her death arose immediately within the dive community. Emails and Web site postings were blistering in their criticism.

Why wasn't there a doctor on the catamaran, one equipped with a defibrillator and intubation kit?

Where was the ambulance, and why wasn't it standing by as a precaution? In fact, as Audrey's body was being carried up the beach on a green plastic lounge chair instead of a stretcher, the top of her wetsuit torn open, witnesses heard the dive team still screaming for someone to find a doctor.

It is generally agreed that somehow the sled malfunctioned. Perhaps the wings placed on the sled for stabilization created a lateral force on the line, slowing it down.

Then there's the question of the oxygen bottle for the lift bag, which failed to inflate correctly. How could this be? Before she began, Pipin opened the valve on the yellow Pony bottle, heard the telltale hiss of air, then closed it again. He assumed it was fully pressurized, but later admits in his book it should have been double-checked with a gauge.

Audrey's body was cremated and Pipin spread her ashes on October 18 in the waters where she often trained, three miles off Miami Beach.

A few days later, October 22 to be exact, Pipin issued a statement which read in part, "After some deliberation, Audrey's parents and I have decided not to disclose any information whatsoever about Audrey's accident and its causes."

In an open letter that attests to his grief-stricken state of mind at the time, Pipin then requested that if a similar accident were to happen to him, relatives and closest friends should ". . . tie me with my weight belt and let me fall into the ocean, with no investigation at all."

Pipin's letter continues, "The best honor that she can receive is to be remembered as the great champion and the great person that she was, and as my most beloved companion."

It took many months for me to be able to function normally without thinking every day about that fateful project in the Dominican Republic. It took even longer for me to escape residual feelings of guilt that perhaps as a sponsor representative, I wasn't at all insistent about safety and emergency medical backup. It's a question that continues to haunt me.

Sled-dog Nightmare

During an exploration career spanning almost twenty-five years, Lonnie Dupre of Grand Marais, Minnesota, has traveled over 14,000 miles through the Arctic and polar regions by dog team, ski, and kayak. His path has often followed in the footsteps of the great explorers of the last century—Robert E. Peary, Roald Amundsen, and Knud Rasmussen, the first to cross the Northwest Passage by dogsled. I met Lonnie in 1989 in Nome, Alaska, during the Bering Bridge Expedition. We drank together in strange bars, traveled with the expedition to its drop-off point in the Soviet Far East, even shared a room. I was there to make them all famous, and he was there to care for and drive the sled dogs.

Striking out on his own in 1991, Lonnie organized and led the Northwest Passage Expedition, the first-ever west-to-east transit of the Canadian Arctic by dogsled, 3,250 miles from Alaska's Prudhoe Bay, to Churchill, Manitoba. It was a brutally harsh trip made all the more unbearable by the deaths of sled dogs and the ensuing outcry from animal rights activists that threatened to end his exploration career forever.

Fifteen of the expedition's sled dogs were lost to dehydration 800 miles into the journey. About thirty miles out of Paulatuk, their own rations almost gone, the men were guided to the safety of a nearby hut by a caribou hunter on a snowmobile.

That year saw little snow on their route between Tuktoyuktuk and Paulatuk, so the team had to follow the ice of the Horton River on what was to be a short overland journey. The river turned into a long, meandering detour that finally cut through a notch in the Smoking Hills, funneling Lonnie and three teammates into Franklin Bay and back onto the Arctic Ocean.

"I recognized that hard traveling in the cold and dark bred frustration and fatigue, and I wondered if somehow our judgment had become clouded," he admitted in early 2009. "The dogs seemed sick. Had the dogs somehow picked up a bug? Perhaps there was something wrong with the food? Were the dogs suffering from a contagious disease and spreading it among themselves? We had lots of questions, but no answers," Lonnie said.

"Looking for an answer, we tried mixing our rations of cheese and butter with their bowls of food. We topped off with water when we could, but that was impossible at the moment because there was no fresh snow available, only salt-laced snow blown in from the ocean."

Lonnie continued his account, "Along the hills, smoke rises from burning sulfur deposits beneath the rock. The hills are steep, averaging a thousand feet in elevation, and run for 100 miles to the east. They were gray, dark, and uninviting. Even the breeze carried the smell of rotten eggs. We talked about crossing the hills to avoid traveling on the bay with its salty ice. But the hills were too steep, and the expedition team too weak. We studied maps, but there was no alternative: we had to cross the bay to the village of Paulatuk—an awful situation to be in, especially since we were all dehydrated and suffering from headaches. I wondered when one of us might stagger and fall."

As their dogs weakened, the mushers jettisoned sleds and equipment to lighten their load.

When news of the deaths got out, the Animal Rights Coalition of the Twin Cities and the Humane Society of the United States went ballistic. "Something is definitely wrong when sled dogs are put through this kind of ordeal for an archaic event," said David Wills, executive vice president of the Humane Society.

Iditarod sled-dog champion Susan Butcher issued a statement, "This is the saddest situation I can think of for a sled dog."

Fellow Minnesotan Paul Schurke, who accompanied Lonnie across the Bering Strait two years before, came to his defense, saying Lonnie was an experienced Arctic traveler who made a mistake and then ran into a bad situation that turned it into a tragedy.

"The margin of error is really slim up there," Schurke told the Minneapolis *Star-Tribune*. "Lonnie apparently got caught in a situation where the margin of error didn't allow for the resources they had, and everybody took a pounding—the men and the dogs—and, unfortunately, some of the dogs died."

Later in the expedition, as Lonnie had time to reflect on the tragedy, he pieced together a more complete explanation. The dogs became dehydrated from licking the salt-laden ice as they ran.

Lonnie admitted he handled the resulting media inquiries poorly. Ann Larkin-Hansen, a team spokesperson, unwittingly led a local Humane Society representative to believe that the use of dogs was basically a publicity stunt to get media attention.

She would subsequently clarify the statement during an interview with the *Star-Tribune*: "What I told her was that they used dogs for several reasons. These guys have lived and worked with dogs all their lives. They love dogs. They love mushing. Yes, the dogs do bring some publicity. But that certainly was not the only reason."

How could Lonnie have handled this differently?

"Have a good spokesperson or manager for the expedition as well as a public relations and marketing person with some experience in crisis management. We had both of these involved but failed to use their services, a huge error."

Lonnie added, "It's a good idea for all expeditions to have a plan in place for the worst possible scenario. Afterwards, try to educate other adventurers about your mishap so they can learn from your mistakes."

To this day, Lonnie continues to warn other mushers about the dangers of salt-laced ice and snow.

Lonnie persevered and went on to conduct a series of flawless expeditions. In 2001 he and teammate, John Hoelscher of Australia, became the first to circumnavigate Greenland, traveling 6,500 miles of the island's rugged coastline by dog team and kayak. In his book, *Greenland Expedition—Where Ice Is Born* (North Word Press, 2000), he would reflect upon his love of the Arctic: "I easily become bored with everyday life. I often long to step back in time, back to the Arctic where life is a bit less complicated and the basic necessities do not include a late-model car."

Reflecting back to his sled-dog nightmare, Lonnie said, "If we knew of every obstacle beforehand, if we were just following a textbook, it wouldn't be an expedition. We wouldn't need to be there."

Final Chapter of an Adventurous Life

Not every project will turn out successfully. This is no *Pirates of the Caribbean* ride you're considering. It's therefore important to anticipate in advance what you'll do if things don't turn out according to plan. Sometimes the best you can do is to hold your head high and gracefully bow out. Consider the 2008 search for adventurer and renowned aviator Steve Fossett.

Fossett was a friend to many of us in The Explorers Club. He was often a guest at the annual dinner, and recipient of The Explorers Club Medal, the Club's highest honor. His disappearance was deeply felt by all who knew him. Personally, I was proud to know he was a reader of *Expedition News*, and had introduced him to one of my daughters at the Waldorf-Astoria dinner where he was honored.

Robert Hyman knew he couldn't sit idly by while Fossett's disappearance continued to mystify the adventure world. A Fellow of the Royal Geographical Society, Life Fellow of The Explorers Club, and acquaintance of Fossett's, Hyman coordinated an extensive twenty-eight-person search during the summer of 2008 that concentrated to the north, where sightings of the adventurer's plane had been reported. A more northerly search zone was consistent with Fossett's plans for when he had intended to return and the amount of fuel the plane carried.

"This is the right thing to do," Hyman said in an interview with the Associated Press at the search team's isolated camp. "Explorers don't leave fellow explorers lost. . . . We want to find out what happened to our friend and colleague, no more and no less."

In preparation for the expedition, Hyman's group conducted over twenty interviews with participants of the previous year's search and carefully reviewed detailed maps and possible travel paths that Fossett may have taken. The team estimates that in all, more than 2,000 hours over eight months went into planning the expedition.

Hyman's team felt they had their bases well covered. Team members consisted of professional high-altitude mountain guides, GPS and mapping specialists, Search and Rescue professionals from two western states, Boy Scout leaders, three pilots, a former Marine Corps Scout Sniper, a mountain climber triathlete, and a senior defense analyst with specialties in search theory and planning, who conducted detailed scenario reconstruction and probability mapping.

Also involved was an expert in the use of balloons carrying camera search equipment. The balloon technology was a new and innovative method to offer a bird's eye view of the search areas. The mobile helium balloons were tethered to a person walking or to a mobile vehicular platform such as a 4x4 or ATV and were equipped with cameras that could detect anomalies in the surrounding terrain.

An advanced mountain base camp was established in an undisclosed location in Nevada's Wassuk Mountains to deploy search teams using a sweep method to cover remote and hard-to-reach areas identified as "high probability" locations of the Fossett aircraft. Team members searched a large area on foot that included three canyons, between 6,000 and 11,000 feet in elevation. The areas searched were carefully recorded with GPS tracks that could be used by others again in the future.

Local authorities were impressed. Hyman's search methodology was highly praised. His team sifted through data obtained by previous searches, utilized a new high-tech NASA computer program that helped visualize the land under a plane's route, and then put "boots on the ground" to trek over the rugged landscape, according to Brendan Riley, who covered the search for the Associated Press.

But it was to no avail. After two weeks of searching, no trace of Steve Fossett was found.

September 2008 marked the final chapter of an extraordinary life when a hiker in rugged eastern California found a pilot's license and other items belonging to Fossett, the holder of more than 100 world records and firsts—including first solo balloon circumnavigation of the globe—who vanished while flying alone in a borrowed plane more than twelve months earlier.

Fossett, sixty-three, disappeared on September 3, 2007, after taking off in a single-engine Citabria Super Decathlon he borrowed from Nevada's Flying M Ranch owned by hotel magnate Barron Hilton. A judge declared Fossett legally dead in February 2008, following a search for the famed aviator that covered 20,000 square miles, reportedly the largest aerial search for a downed plane in U.S. history.

Hyman and his team had returned from their unsuccessful search when news came that a sporting goods store manager named Preston Morrow, accompanied by his trusty Australian sheepdog Kona, found an identity card, a pilot's license, a third ID, and $1,005 in muddy cash tangled in a bush off a trail just west of Mammoth Lakes. He turned the items in to local police after unsuccessful attempts to contact Fossett's family.

Shortly afterward, a team of police and rescue workers found the wreckage of the plane a quarter-mile away; it appeared to have hit the mountainside head-on, authorities said. Most of the plane's fuselage disintegrated on impact, and the engine was found several hundred feet away at an elevation of 9,700 feet. Experts agreed Fossett likely died on impact. His tennis shoes and driver's license were later found—both with animal bite marks on them according to the Associated Press.

For Hyman, the question was what to do when hundreds, perhaps thousands were pinning their hopes on your search methodology and high-tech equipment? When his expedition returned without any evidence of Fossett's disappearance, Hyman acknowledged that the ultimate goal was not fame and fortune for the search team, but the resolution of a mystery that had perplexed the adventure world for over a year.

In an official statement released in October 2008, Hyman said, "We conducted an extensive search this past August-September out of respect and reverence for our friend and colleague Steve Fossett. While we did not succeed in locating his crash site, and we are saddened by the outcome, we are relieved that Mr. Fossett's plane has been found."

Hyman continued, "The most important thing was to find out what happened to Mr. Fossett. We want to thank all who gave so generously of their time and expertise to this search, which included those in the other search parties, federal agencies, state and local officials, and the many who assisted us with information, advice and logistical support. Our sincerest condolences go out to the Fossett family."

In November 2008, DNA analysis of bone fragments discovered a half mile from where the adventurer's plane crashed were positively identified as belonging to the body of the millionaire aviator. Authorities declined to say what bones were found to avoid causing the family further anguish.

Waterworld

For a time, any adventure sponsorship sent to the Du Pont Company would land on my desk—we counted 1,200 in one year alone. When you're bombarded with that many proposals, it's difficult to look at more than the first few paragraphs and flip through the photos and maps. One outlandish sponsorship opportunity stood out above the others, not because it was appropriate for Du Pont, but because of the audacity of the concept . . . and a particularly glaring typographical error.

Reid Stowe, a professional New York painter and sculptor, dreamed of accomplishing a seagoing feat never before achieved in the history of mankind. Similar to some of my favorite expeditions up to that time and since then, his proposal had a simple, self-descriptive name: 1,000 Days at Sea.

Reid, a tall veteran sailor with Caribbean blue eyes and hair pulled into a tight ponytail, planned to become the first human to remain on a boat for 1,000 days, without resupply and out of sight of land, "longer than anyone since the human race evolved out of the sea," he promised.

It would be a historic project, and one for the record books. One thousand days at sea. It would dwarf history's best-known sea stories, including the abandoned crew of the *H.M.S. Bounty* set adrift in 1789 for forty-eight days in a twenty-three-foot boat, and the wretched souls of the whale ship *Essex* rammed by an angry bull sperm whale in 1820, setting crew members adrift in harpoon boats for almost 100 days. In 1988, five Costa Rican fishermen were blown to sea in a twenty-nine-foot motorboat that drifted across the Pacific Ocean for five months and 4,500 miles without resupply, an account retold in *Five Against the Sea* by Ron Arias (Thorndike Press, 1990). A tough 142-day voyage, yes. Still nothing compared with Reid's plan to stay afloat seven times longer.

Reid's project would be analogous to a space voyage to Mars, which had some executives at NASA unofficially monitoring his progress. I was intrigued, but knew it wasn't right for Du Pont. For one thing, if one of a thousand things went wrong before day 657 (which was the previous record set in 1986–88), I felt the record attempt would sink, perhaps even taking Reid and the boat with it.

Still, I couldn't take my eyes off his proposal, especially considering his handwritten cover note in which he consistently referred to the project as an "expidition." His typo got my attention. Usually, spelling and grammar count when you're seeking expedition funding for the trip of your dreams. Sponsors need to know you have the communication skills to report back to their sales force, retail buyers, the media, and consumers without misspelling their brand name.

Determined to meet him if for no other reasons than to work on his spelling, I visited Reid on his hand-built seventy-foot gaff-rigged schooner, the *Anne*, located in Chelsea, along New York's West Side Highway. While his New Agey, metaphysical talk about tracing the outline of an imaginary sea turtle on the sea failed to resonate with my pragmatic business sense, and his shipboard carvings of mermaids, dragon heads, and sea horses looked liked they belonged on the *20,000 Leagues Under the Sea* ride at Walt Disney World, it didn't matter. Having worked with experienced explorers, dreamers, and schemers of all types, I believed he had the passion and commitment to pull it off.

If there were a marathon for expidition, er, expedition planning, Stowe would be wearing a winner's wreath. From the time he first dreamed up his project in 1986 to the day he logged the first of his 1,000 days, twenty-one years passed. During the planning phase, Reid took friends, supporters, and potential sponsors on an evening sail once or twice a week. He explained to me how he and a tall, lithe Frenchwoman named Laurence Guillem, who would eventually become his third wife, would take every precaution to ensure a safe voyage.

Desalinators and rain would provide fresh water, he explained; solar energy and water generators driven by the forward motion of the ship would power his lights and satellite communications. For food, sprouts would be grown; meals would include pasta, dried beans, nuts, grain and rice; and the two would fish in between their daily chores, ship maintenance, exercise, and blogging. If rescue was required, he could summon help with an emergency EPIRB unit that would send a distress signal to a satellite, then to search and rescue aircraft that could home in on the *Anne's* exact position.

I listened patiently, but all I could think about was the possibility that Laurence would become pregnant. A pregnant wife would mean a baby in nine months, and a baby would likely mean the need for outside medical support. End of trip. Reid assured me that the two of them would be taking an ample supply of contraceptives along.

"Great," I thought to myself. "Then if the boat flounders on a reef somewhere off Bora Bora, they can inflate 1,000 condoms and float to safety. Or use them as water wings. Or whatever."

Here was a guy who was going to eat mostly fish for the entire journey. I was sure that by day 1,000 he would not only be eating fish, but might even wind up talking to fish by the time the project was over, driven insane by the ceaseless monotony.

Reid set sail with Laurence from France on a 100-day shakedown cruise in 1994, sailing south to the equator, then north to New York. He would later wax poetic in a gushy society-page wedding story in the *New York Times*, "A man and a woman sailing away together on a boat is the stuff of mythology, the stuff of poetry, the stuff of rock-and-roll songs. There are extremely beautiful moments, like being woken up in the morning by singing whales."

Laurence didn't quite see it that way, soon realizing she wasn't cut out to be a floating guinea pig. Their relationship eventually sank as Reid doggedly continued to pursue his seagoing experiment in self-sufficiency.

In April 2007, Reid, then fifty-five, set sail with someone new, twenty-three-year-old girlfriend and novice sailor, Soanya Ahmad. They departed from Weehawken, New Jersey, thanks to the generosity of dozens of product sponsors and individual contributors.

On day fifteen the *Anne* had a serious collision with a freighter that damaged the boat's bowsprit and forward rigging. By that December, caught in the "Roaring Forties" in the South Indian Ocean, the *Anne* lost both foresail and mainsail. But that was the least of their worries.

By February 2008, Soanya was becoming incapacitated by crippling bouts of nausea in the rough seas of the southern ocean. She experienced loss of appetite, weight loss, and apathy. This was a woman after my own heart, I thought. While I don't have any logical excuse for seasickness, other than it's part of my DNA, Soanya had the best reason of all: it was morning sickness. She was pregnant. With the help of a local yacht club, on day 306 off Fremantle, Western Australia, Reid arranged for an at-sea transfer that would allow him to continue his voyage alone.

"The next bit of land after Australia . . . who even knows where that is? That was my chance to get off, and I took it," Soanya explained in a feature story that appeared in the New York *Daily News* in July 2008.

Reid believes that Soanya's voyage on the *Anne* was the longest unsupported voyage by a man and woman in history, and that Soanya now holds the record for the longest consecutive time at sea for a woman. Record or not, it was quite an accomplishment. She gave birth five months later to a boy named Darshen, who was conceived at sea. Reid plans to return to New York in 2010, back to Soanya and the child he has yet to meet. He would blog, "They are not the first woman and child to wait for their man to come home from the sea. It is the most ancient of stories."

Reid broke the 657-day record in early February 2009 near Cape Horn, suffering a knockdown from a rogue wave in the process. He was slightly hurt, a sail was lost, and water flooded the cabin. Yet undeterred, he continues on his longest nonstop sea voyage in history and a berth in the record books.

When Things Don't Go Quite as Planned

☞ **There's No Such Thing as "No Comment"**—It's difficult to conduct interviews when calls on your satellite phone are costing $7 per minute. Fully brief a spokesperson back home, then have him or her respond to media requests. Your spokesperson can also screen inquiries, allowing you to choose which reporter, producer, or freelance writer you want to respond to directly from the field. Then be sure to anticipate all the tough questions and think carefully in advance about your answers.

Be proactive, not reactive. That way you have a better chance that your bad news will be on page one for just one day, rather than several. Say as much as you can and offer additional information once more is known. If the media believe you're trying to cover anything up, the story will linger.

When things go wrong, issue a statement, even a short one. Just don't fall into the trap of saying "no comment," which makes it seem as if you're hiding something. You or your spokesperson should say you're investigating the incident, say you're cooperating with authorities, say something positive to show how you're responding to the situation. Tell the truth. No one likes a liar. What's more, be sure not to say anything to the media you'll later regret, as I did. . . .

As a public relations pro, I should have known better. I was caught with my own pants down, speaking to the *New York Times* a bit too enthusiastically when asked about Will Steger's Trans-Antarctica Expedition in 1989.

"Antarctica is the hot continent now," I said rather breathlessly. "Mount Everest is out. It's been done every which way. It's been trashed." I was referring to recent news about mounds of garbage at Everest base camp, but it didn't come out well. I was mortified: elsewhere in the same issue, my admittedly flip comment became the *Times*' Quotation of the Day.

A few days later, I was further humiliated to learn that my statement became the subject of an entire column by *Times* columnist Tom Wicker, titled "Trashing the Antarctic." Bemoaning the corporate sponsorship of Steger's ambitious project, he saw the adventure as a thinly veiled attempt to "promote dog food, freeze-dried soup, and the latest in wash-it-yourself parkas or lightweight tundra boots." My comment that Steger would become "a true American hero, a household name, by the time this thing is over," only fueled Wicker's ire.

Ouch. Lesson learned: get your brain in gear before placing mouth in motion.

☞ **Develop a Contingency Plan**—Setbacks are inevitable. Think ahead and decide in advance how you will handle a team member's severe injury or death. Who will you notify? What steps will you take to mitigate the situation? Compile contact information for next of kin, law enforcement authorities, search and rescue organizations, and your main sponsors, who should hear bad news directly from you, not read about it first in news coverage.

☞ **Update Your Web Site or Blog Daily**—The Web is your single best means of communicating to the outside world. Reporters and editors will turn to your Web site or blog and quote it frequently, so make sure information about the expedition's situation is posted daily.

☞ **Safety First, Sponsors Second**—Duofold, the base layer manufacturer, sponsored Canadian climber Roger Marshall who died after apparently slipping on blue ice while attempting Everest's Hornbein Couloir in 1987. It's believed Marshall may have felt undue pressure to deliver on all of his sponsorship commitments, and may have taken some unnecessary risks. Be very clear with your sponsors in advance that safety comes first. There's no value to a sponsor if their adventurer comes back dead, or not at all.

☞ **Insure Yourself**—Protect yourself from an unfortunate turn of events by purchasing emergency medical transportation assistance. Comprehensive policies for medical care and medical evacuation, as well as trip cancellation and interruption insurance, typically cost 5 to 7 percent of the total trip expense. Join the American Alpine Club and receive 5 percent off the cost of a policy with Global Rescues (globalrescue.com). Sites that offer side-by-side comparison and prices are: insuremytrip.com, squaremouth.com, and totaltravelinsurance.com.

Other resources to consider:

Medex Global Group—medexassist.com

MedjetAssist—medjetassist.com

U.S. Travel Insurance Association—ustia.org

You're Not Done Yet

The project is over. You've been covered in newspapers nation-wide and are on a first-name basis with *The Today Show*'s Matt Lauer. But even if you've returned home dog tired, deep in debt, and have a wicked case of trench foot, you're not done yet. Not if you ever hope to find someone to pay for another trip in the future. It's time to sharpen your people skills and take a tip from the late Edward "Ned" Gillette.

Ned Gillette was an explorer's explorer. An author, photographer, lecturer, design consultant, and former member of the 1968 U.S. Olympic Cross-Country Ski Team, he even looked like an explorer with his dark raccoon tan, deep intense eyes, and weathered complexion creased by years in the sun. In 1981, the career adventurer was best known for the Everest Grand Circle, an offbeat 300-mile circumnavigation of Everest with an average altitude of 20,000 feet. Many criticized him for accepting sponsorship money from Camel cigarettes, but for him the ends justified the means.

Ned's dream to row across the fierce Drake Passage between Cape Horn and Antarctica nearly killed him in 1987 when heavy pack ice blocked the route. In light of his last name, it was hard to resist writing about his "close shave" in press releases that we issued about our client's sponsorship.

The Drake is one mother of a body of water, named for Sir Francis Drake who in the sixteenth century called it ". . . the most mad seas."

When the cold air of the Antarctica ice cap collides with the warmer maritime air over the ocean surrounding the continent, the result is a vicious storm belt of blizzards and dense fog spanning 600 miles from the southern tip of South America to the South Shetland Islands. On the best of days the ocean is turbulent and, on the worst of days, impassable in smaller vessels. Mariners have long called this region the "Roaring Forties," "Furious Fifties," and "Screaming Sixties," referring not to decades, but lines of latitude. If you're not wealthy enough to fly to Antarctica, the only way to cross the fierce Antarctic Convergence is by ship. Sometimes you can luck out and seas will be relatively calm, what they call the "Drake Lake." But don't count on it. Usually, it's the "Drake Shake."

Students on Ice, which has organized educational expeditions to the continent for ten years, advises there's no magic cure to fight seasickness on Drake crossings. Students and chaperones alike try bands, patches, and pills, staring at the horizon, and eating ginger, with varying degrees of success. Like the famous line in *Jaws*—"We're going to need a bigger boat"—when it comes to ocean crossings for those prone to seasickness, no boat is too big. The only real cure is to get through the passage to calmer waters.

Now imagine a treacherous journey in a twenty-eight-foot rowboat, and you get a sense of why sponsors might want to tag along to demonstrate how their products perform in such an extreme environment. It's the halo effect again: if that waterproof and breathable parka works in the Drake Passage, it'll certainly provide adequate protection to those whose seafaring adventures are limited to commuting on the Staten Island Ferry.

In March 1988, Ned, then forty-three, and his team set out against the currents, fueled by 6,000 calories per day of energy bars and shakes. On the first day, *Sea Tomato*'s small sail caught a ferocious northwesterly wind. "Gusts were up to 50 knots," Ned told *Sports Illustrated*'s Robert

Sullivan. "We capsized three different times, and one of us went over-board each time."

Sullivan writes: "At least the savage winds blew *Sea Tomato* in the right direction. She covered 90 nautical miles the first two days, and Gillette's crew didn't use their oars until the third day out. The going continued to be rough as heavy squalls tossed the 1,500-pound boat like . . . well, a tomato." For fourteen days, the four-man team muscled their hardy heavy-gauge aluminum *Sea Tomato* 684 miles from Cape Horn to Nelson Island in the South Shetlands, just off the Antarctica peninsula. Ever the deal-maker, Gillette traded the *Sea Tomato* to the Chilean navy for a flight back to Punta Arenas.

Ned later organized the East-West Express, journeying 4,000 miles across Asia along Marco Polo's Silk Road in much the same self-sufficient manner Marco himself might have done it. In fact, it was the first modern-day crossing of Asia by traditional camel caravan. Sponsored in large part by Polartec, in December 1993, midway into the trip, he reported to *Outside* magazine, "We walk, we sleep, we eat, read or write, but true entertainment is playing with camels, Aardvark and Collie."

Exploring was a business for Ned. He viewed sponsorship as vital to the success of his projects. "Big ideas cost big money," he said. Each trip, he knew, was an opportunity to create a documentary or a coffee-table book, be paid to charm a slide-show audience, or schedule an outdoor store appearance. He would do anything to maximize the value a sponsor received through its support of each project. Schedule most explorers on television, and they suddenly suffer from selective amnesia when it comes to mentioning their sponsors. Ned was refreshingly different. He'd plug his heaviest bankrollers half a dozen times and make it seem painless, effortless.

"He was first in a growing breed of modern adventurers who recognized that what mattered for the contemporary adventurer was not just skill and intrepidity, but style, flair, finesse," says writer and filmmaker Jon Bowermaster in *Wildebeest in a Rainstorm* (Menasha Ridge Press, 2009).

Ned knew that crediting the major sources of his funding was not only the right thing to do to maintain his nomadic lifestyle, but he also believed that once a sponsor, always a sponsor—if he played his cards right, the company might well become a source of future funding. Prior to a pitch meeting with Reebok and Malden Mills in 1991, he told me, "I've always believed that the kind of sponsorship I like is a very personal relationship that starts because a company likes us and vice versa."

I called Paige Boucher to reminisce. Paige is a well-known outdoor-industry public relations executive living the dream life and a dream career with her family in Steamboat Springs, Colorado.

"Ned made my job fun," she said. "I was brand new, a lowly designer at The North Face who was sent to the backwoods of Minnesota to help Ned evaluate expedition garments.

"We were all staying in a tiny motel with no phones out in the middle of nowhere, driving around in a used minivan, but Ned was full of good humor. Many outdoor adventurers I work with are so full of themselves—it's all about them all the time. But Ned wanted to get to know me as a person. We laughed the entire time."

As soon as Ned left on one adventure, he was already thinking about the next. Sponsors like 3M, Burlington Industries, Eastern Airlines, and Sony lined up to provide him with gear and cash if he would wear their logos, test their products, take stunning photographs of said products in action, then visit with factory workers, sales reps, and retail buyers. He was a fixture at the outdoor-industry trade shows, often appearing for The North Face.

Later he would go on to explore other regions of the world before meeting a tragic end in the mountains of Pakistan. In 1998, while sleeping next to his wife, former 1976 U.S. Olympic Alpine Ski Team member

Susie Patterson, then forty-two, Ned was brutally shotgunned in their tent. He died the next day at the age of fifty-three. Susie was wounded by approximately seventy buckshot pellets in her back and side, but survived in part because Ned summoned the strength to lunge at the assailant with a rock. The tragedy occurred just after Ned's latest expedition, the circumnavigation of 26,660-foot Nanga Parbat, the world's sixth highest mountain.

Recalling Ned's diverse adventure career, John Fry would write in *Ski* magazine, "After all that, Ned's death in a bungled shotgun robbery was as improbable as Clint Eastwood slipping on a banana peel in Last Chance Gulch."

More recently, Paige Boucher added, "He was so sincere and so genuine, I knew he was truly interested in people on a personal level, not just business. He made it so much more than a business relationship. This made us more inclined to support him the next time he came around. "Here it is twenty years later, and I've moved on to Mountain Hardwear, yet I know that if Ned were still alive, we'd be having fun together promoting his latest adventure."

Ned was a superb public speaker. As he recounted his various adventures, crediting his sponsors every time, you could hear a pin drop in the room. Seaborn "Beck" Weathers, the Dallas pathologist who almost froze to death on Mount Everest in 1996, had a similar talent to enthrall an audience. His very physical appearance—right arm amputated halfway below the elbow, four fingers and the thumb on his left hand removed, reconstructed nose—attested to the horrors he faced during that fateful season on the mountain.

Weathers and celebrated climber Yasuko Namba, the second Japanese woman to summit the Seven Summits, were found by rescuers at

9 a.m., Saturday, May 11, 1996, then left there, considered too far gone to be revived. They had neither tent nor sleeping bag. Namba died, but amazingly, Weathers revived himself hours later.

David Breashears, on Everest with an IMAX film crew, said in a *PBS NOVA* documentary that Weathers, then fifty, staggered toward camp like an apparition, face blackened by the extreme cold, and frostbitten hands outstretched like a scarecrow's.

"It's a ghost, it has to be. This person is dead," Breashears related. "But he's decided he wants to live. He's our miracle. It's one great inspirational story in the tragedy."

I attended a presentation by Weathers a few years after his ordeal. During his speech, "Miracle on Everest," Weathers recounted his tale of survival and the lessons he learned from his second chance at life, focusing on the importance of perseverance and maintaining a positive attitude. The experience obviously still haunted him as his voice broke while recounting the heroism of the helicopter pilot who plucked Weathers from 19,200 feet in one of the highest helicopter rescues in history. Strong stuff indeed.

~~⊙~~

Another explorer who consistently generates revenue in the low- to mid-five figures per talk is Erik Weihenmayer, arguably the world's best-known blind athlete. In May 2001, Erik, who lost his sight at age thirteen due to retinoschesis, a degenerative disease that detaches and splits retinas, joined the National Federation of the Blind Allegra 2001 Everest Expedition and became the only blind person in history to reach the summit of Everest.

Time magazine called it one of the greatest sporting achievements of 2001, honoring his "blind faith" by placing him on its cover in June 2001.

A little over a year later, when he stood on top of Mount Kosciusko in Australia, he completed his seven-year quest to climb all the Seven Summits. Since then he has appeared in documentary TV programs, organized "No Barriers" events for disabled athletes, competed in adventure races, and taught mountaineering and rock climbing to blind students in Tibet. Erik's Emmy-nominated film about his historic Everest climb, *Farther Than the Eye Can See,* continues to successfully raise thousands of dollars for numerous charities.

Working with the public relations agency CGPR, I hired Erik to speak at a W.L. Gore & Associates breakfast during the Outdoor Retailer trade show in Salt Lake. The purpose of the presentation was to help Gore maintain awareness among retail store buyers of outdoor garments containing Gore-Tex fabric.

What makes a presentation by Erik even more memorable than his message of turning every adversity, major or minor, into a genuine advantage, is his use of humor. He says being a blind climber is like being a Jamaican bobsledder, "The words don't connect in people's minds."

He explains that he wanted to be considered a working member of the Everest team. "No way was I going to be carried to the top and spiked like a football."

At one point he holds up a one-dollar bill and explains that being totally blind requires that he adopt special skills.

"Can anyone identify money by smell?"

He pauses for effect as the entire audience contemplates the possibility that he can actually smell the difference between a buck and a sawbuck.

"Well, neither can I," he jokes.

Erik likes to talk about the "Even I" syndrome. It goes like this: At many presentations someone in the audience would invariably walk up and say, "Man, I think that's so incredible what you did. Even I with two perfectly working eyes couldn't make it up Everest."

Erik would laugh to himself, take it as a compliment, but think that here's a guy who lives in Orlando and smokes a pack of cigarettes a day. He says it's like, "Dude, do you think the difference between success and failure has to do with perfectly working eyes? You're seventy years old, you're in Orlando, you've never walked more than a mile in your life. What makes you think you could climb a mountain with perfectly working eyes? It goes well beyond that."

Explorers and adventurers have a responsibility to return home safely and share their experiences with those of us who never left the comfort of our homes. Attending these presentations, studying timing, content, and key messages, then frequent rehearsals can help anyone become memorable speakers themselves.

Make Sure They Don't Forget You

☞ **Submit a Wrap-up Report**—As soon as possible upon your return, summarize the trip and include copies of all the newspaper, magazine, Web site and blog coverage you can find. Google Alerts can do this for you at no cost. For a cost ranging in the low hundreds of dollars, you can also track TV and radio exposure through companies such as the Video Monitoring Service (VMS), which monitors television newscasts in 210 U.S. markets. They can provide a run-down of every television or cable news program that mentions your project. From there, you can order copies of the segments to download to any computer, or actual DVDs of the segments.

Through a similar service, Du Pont estimated their sponsorship of the 1986 North Pole Expedition netted 4,000 newspaper articles for a combined 90 million impressions. The exposure resulted in 240 million brand impressions through media coverage that would have cost $6.7 million if purchased as advertising. What's more, it showcased Du Pont products in the best possible light.

A few years later, the company's support of the Trans-Antarctica Expedition generated 4.7 billion brand impressions worldwide, representing another excellent return on their investment. The project was so massive that expedition exposure included a series of prime-time specials on ABC, and its own song written by jazz musician Grover Washington, Jr.

☞ **Meet With Product Designers**—While the project is still fresh in everyone's mind, submit a detailed evaluation of the sponsor's product used in the field. Explain how well it performed and how you'd suggest making further improvements. Then offer to present your findings in person.

Will Steger, for instance, provided feedback that helped Lands' End, the retail catalog company, develop better clothing for people to wear in the cold.

In 2007, Coleman Exponent tents, stoves, sleeping bags, headlamps, lanterns, and backpacks protected mountaineer and Denver middle schoolteacher Mike Haugen on a successful expedition to Mount Everest. Afterward, Mike filed detailed field reports for review by Coleman product managers and the company's product development lab. Just as Tang breakfast drink went on the early NASA moon missions, Coleman subjected its gear to the kind of real-world testing they could never achieve in a lab.

☞ **Give Thanks**—Adventurers and explorers are notorious for forgetting about their sponsors once the project is over. If you ever dream of going on another sponsored trip, or even if you don't, thank your sponsors once, twice, as many times as you can. Too much gratitude is never enough. Send them a rock from Antarctica, prayer flags from Nepal, a patch that accompanied you on a dive to the *Titanic*, perhaps an Inuit soapstone carving—any meaningful memento will do so long as it's not another ball cap or T-shirt.

Sometimes, expedition souvenirs presented to sponsors can backfire despite your best intentions. Used cold-weather clothing from the 1989–90 Trans-Antarctica Expedition was returned to W.L. Gore & Associates at the conclusion of the expedition. The bag of unwashed parkas worn by explorers—men whose idea of bathing consisted of quickly rubbing snow on their briefly naked bodies—remained lost in storage for at least five years. Seems Gore was looking to build a museum display to celebrate twenty years of Gore-Tex, their ubiquitous waterproof breathable laminate, but they simply forgot about it.

"Unfortunately, no one remembered to wash the clothing and the dog vest before storage," Gore associate Lisa Wyre told *Expedition News*. "After I opened the bag and realized what happened, I closed it immediately. The smell lingered for hours." Wyre says the most interesting findings were an eyeglass case, knit purple hat, notes on scraps of paper, and tissues in various stages of use.

"While we didn't have to call in the Hazmat guys in rubber gloves, the clothes could have practically walked away under their own power."

☞ **Schedule Personal Appearances and Speaking Engagements**—In advance of your trip, schedule a specific number of appearance days on behalf of your main sponsors. You may, for instance, offer three to five appearance days, plus expenses, as part of the sponsorship, then charge a per diem of $1,000 to $1,500 thereafter, with your expenses paid in addition (don't be a pig about it, travel coach just like your sponsor probably travels). Use appearance days to visit the factory workers who made your gear and apparel; attend sales meetings; meet with retail buyers; conduct educational PowerPoint presentations at schools; and take the sponsor's best customers on hikes and other soft outdoor adventures.

For Hill's Pet Products, Will Steger trekked to dog shows, radio and TV interviews, and a convention of 6,000 veterinarians in Texas—all payback for their support. For 3M he hosted a standing-room-only cocktail reception at the Outdoor Retailer convention themed, "Chill with Will."

Public speaking can also become a source of future revenue. For instance, in 1982 Laurie Skreslet became the first Canadian to climb Mount Everest. Since then, while continuing to climb, he's become a successful motivational speaker who teaches business, leadership, and challenge courses in the Canadian Rockies. He's spoken in front of over 500,000 people for companies such as Canada Life, Du Pont, Fidelity, Novartis, and Sprint, has written a best-selling book, *To The Top of Everest* (Kids Can Press, 2001), and still has a booking agent who commands approximately $10,000 per talk.

American climber Ed Viestur's public presentations are so successful, held in venues that hold a thousand people, that they've been called the "Grateful Ed Tour," according to *Outside* magazine. It's during these talks that Ed explains that when it comes to mountain climbing, "Getting up is optional. Getting down is mandatory. It's gotta be a round trip."

☞ **Write a Book, Then Appear on *Oprah*—**While not the most lucrative endeavor an adventurer or explorer can pursue, a book provides another way to credit sponsors and adds enormous credibility the next time you seek funding.

Minnesota explorer Dan Buettner, leader of the 1995 MayaQuest expedition through Central America, has come a long way since then. Joining the ranks of the country's most famous authors, Dan made a television appearance on *The Oprah Winfrey Show* in 2008 to promote his book, *Blue Zones* (National Geographic, 2008), which reveals the nine secrets of the world's longest-lived people.

The appearance worked wonders for marketing his book. "I figure the *Oprah Show* boosted my sales in the tens of thousands. Book sales soared to number one on the Amazon.com Healthy Living list and spawned a major order from Target stores. It also yielded several speaking appearances, TV offers, and offers to license the Blue Zones brand."

Dan is often amazed at the woman's clout.

"At a recent speech, the person who introduced me mentioned my three Guinness World Records for cycling five continents.

"Silence.

"My Emmy Award for Africatrek.

"Silence. One guy yawned.

"The Quest series that let more than 20 million kids direct fifteen expeditions.

"More silence.

"The National Magazine finalist award for the *National Geographic* story.

"Some bored shuffling.

"An appearance on *Oprah*.

"At that, the crowd erupted with an impressed 'oooh.'"

Sharing some quality couch time with Oprah is one of the most difficult achievements in book publishing, but it is possible, as Dan has shown. How do you break through to the Queen of Daytime TV? It's a long shot, but one way to meet the Big O is to click "Be on the Show" at oprah.com.

A good source of information about how to write a book proposal is the book about pitching books called, not surprisingly, *Book Proposals That Sell* by W. Terry Whalin (Write Now Publications, 2005).

☞ **Plan Ahead**—You've just pulled off an amazing adventure and the cameras are all pointed your way. "What's next?" you'll likely be asked. You should always be thinking one or two projects ahead. Don't just bask in the limelight; use your fifteen minutes of fame to begin building support for your next project. In fact, if you can, announce your next project while everyone still remembers who you are, before the honeymoon is over.

Dream Up the Trip of a Lifetime

IF YOUR PLANS FOR THE TRIP OF A LIFETIME ARE WELL AT HAND, THEN you're halfway home. But if you believe in your heart of hearts that there's something out there calling your name, something pulling you to travel and explore, but you're not sure quite where, this chapter will point you in new directions. Or at least it will provide a fascinating look at how others have responded to the siren call of adventure.

The Name Game

Those who want to go somewhere and aren't keen on paying for it themselves need to answer the "So what?" question with a good hook, and especially a great, unforgettable name. Something that sounds interesting, perhaps a bit offbeat. A name that will make sponsors, the media, and armchair explorers everywhere want to learn more, and then follow along vicariously.

For example, two of my favorite project names are:

Death Valley to Denali—In 1997, Sean Tracy, then thirty-two, traveled by mountain bike from Death Valley National Monument, the lowest point in North America at 282 feet below sea level, to the continent's highpoint of 20,320 feet on Mount McKinley. Few of the stories in *Expedition News* have ever elicited as much interest from readers. For three months, Sean, a carpenter from New Hope, Pennsylvania, experienced his dream expedition, without sponsors, without Internet links, and without fanfare, paying the $9,000 in expenses out of his own wages.

Accompanied by a friend, Alicia Ellingsworth, twenty-nine, who drove a Toyota Land Cruiser support vehicle, Sean left the Badwater Basin low point on March 21, 1997, on a mountain bike, then headed up the eastern side of the Sierra Nevada through eastern California, proceeded to the northern part of the state, crossed into central Oregon, central Washington, then British Columbia, the Yukon, and on to Talkeetna, Alaska, arriving at the staging area for McKinley on May 22.

Meeting up with three climbing partners, he maintained the human-powered objective of his project by bushwhacking forty miles over treacherous glaciated terrain—a dangerously crevassed route that most explorers prefer to reach by air. On June 21, after eleven days on the approach and fourteen days on the mountain's West Buttress route, after biking and hiking 3,611 miles, Sean Tracy stood atop McKinley, reportedly becoming the first to travel under human power from North America's low point to its highest. Today Sean has a company in Bucks County, Pennsylvania, that converts old timber-frame barns into custom homes and is dreaming about another climbing and biking expedition.

Grease to Greece Rally—In 2008, ten teams drove from London to Greece powered only by waste vegetable oil scavenged from restaurants and burger bars along the way. The team, led by Andy Pag, a freelance TV producer and journalist from Croyden, South London, drove 2,330 miles from London to Greece, filling the tanks of their modified diesels from French fry cookers, schnitzel shops, and roadside bus stops south through Europe—in an effort to get people to use sustainable fuels every day.

During this cleverly named "fat finding" mission, some teams were running on pure grease, while others brewed up biodiesel from the fat they collected on the way to Athens. The year before, Andy and his mates completed a 4,000-mile carbon negative expedition to Timbuktu, Mali, in a chocolate-powered truck—oil from cocoa butter was the main ingredient. Over 150 people who followed along online signed the team's "Greasy Pledge," which reads, "If these idiots can make it to Greece without using fossil fuels, I'll make my next tank fossil fuel free."

Forever the punster, Andy is toying with yet another play on words for an upcoming expedition. "Grease is the World" he plans to call it.

It's a big world out there. In fact, with space tourism on the near horizon, it's getting even bigger. There are plenty of projects to consider either joining or launching on your own. Here are a few to consider:

Solve a Mystery
What Ever Happened to Amelia Earhart?

The International Group for Historic Aircraft Recovery (TIGHAR) is on a tireless search for Amelia Earhart, the famous pilot nicknamed "Lady Lindy," who disappeared over seventy years ago somewhere in the Pacific. In 1937, at the height of her fame, she vanished while attempting to fly around the world with navigator Fred Noonan. Their fate is one of the twentieth century's greatest mysteries. Historical records led the search to Nikumaroro, an uninhabited atoll in the Republic of Kiribati, where the partial skeleton of a castaway, uncovered in 1940, was thought to be of a person of Northern European descent of about Earhart's height. But it wasn't a complete set of bones; a portion of the skeleton was taken by coconut crabs (a.k.a. "robber" crabs) known to return to their underground burrows with food.

Robber crabs are the world's largest land crabs and can crack coconuts with their strong pincers. TIGHAR tests with animal carcasses on Nikumaroro in 2001 and 2007 confirm that the meat and bones disappear in a matter of days. Remote-control photo and video cameras showed robber crabs, which live to be seventy years old, were among the culprits. "If we can find the bones that the crabs took, we may have our 'smoking gun,'" said TIGHAR expedition leader Ric Gillespie. For a fee of $50,000, for which you'll need sponsorship or pay yourself, you can gain great experience while helping TIGHAR continue looking for large well-established crab burrows and perhaps for the actual crabs, or their relatives, who may have eaten the famed aviatrix (tighar.org).

Does the U.S. Loch Ness Monster Really Exist?

It's America's version of the Loch Ness monster, a sea creature said to reside in Lake Champlain, between New York and Vermont. Frequently during the summer months, expeditions involving dozens of participants and sophisticated surveillance gear camp along the shoreline to find the mysterious creature.

Researchers theorize that Champ could be anything from a plesiosaur to a large sturgeon. Most agree there would have to be a breeding colony of the creatures in the lake for them to survive over the years.

If you have the funding, Ruby Anderson of Champ Expedition in Naugatuck, Connecticut, might let you join her group, which is usually headquartered at Button Bay State Park and Campground near Vergennes, Vermont, where there have been several sightings (champexpedition2008.bravehost.com).

Find Something

Icelanders Go Back to the Seventies

Within sight of the sheer, towering walls that millions of puffins call home, volunteers and researchers are uncovering the remains of 417 properties lost when Heimaey, a small town off the coast of Iceland, was destroyed by a volcanic eruption in 1973. The natural disaster covered one-third of the community in up to twenty meters of lava and ash. Kristin Johannsdottir is leading a modern-day archaeological effort to uncover a section of town where the homes were steam boiled in hot ash, yet left mainly intact. Clothes still hang in closets as they did almost forty years ago. Dishes line the cupboards. It's as if nothing changed since the 1970s, except the lives of Icelanders displaced by this modern-day Pompeii.

While homeowners were reimbursed for their property by the government, personal items such as photos and heirlooms found in some of the lightly damaged structures will be returned.

"The people of Heimaey are pretty excited about the entire project," Johannsdottir says. Over the course of several years, they hope to create a historical exhibit—a reconstructed town under a large roof—to show how people lived in 1973. The project is expected to cost about $2.3 million. Here's an idea: volunteer to help uncover what remains of the homes of Heimaey. Digs will continue into 2010 and beyond (pompeinordursins.is).

Where is Roald Amundsen's South Pole Tent?

British Capt. Robert F. Scott (1868–1912) vowed he would not race to the South Pole to be first. Nonetheless, he was bitterly disappointed when he arrived at the bottom of the world on Jan. 18, 1912, only to find a tent, a Norwegian flag, and a letter to the King of Norway left more than a month earlier by the Norwegian explorer Roald Amundsen (1872–1928). The day Scott reached the South Pole he famously wrote in his diary, "Great God! This is an awful place and terrible enough for us to have laboured to it without the reward of priority."

On their way back from the South Pole, Scott's expedition perished in a blizzard just eleven miles short of their food and fuel cache. A geologist to the very end, Scott and his men were found with a sledge packed with thirty-five pounds of ordinary rocks and very few supplies.

Finding Amundsen's lightweight canvas tent was a dream of Colonel Norman D. Vaughan, who wanted to locate it with ice-penetrating radar and bring it to Norway for the 1994 Olympic Winter Games in Lillehammer. It is believed the tent, topped by a Norwegian flag and a pennant from the ship *Fram*, is now about fifty feet below the surface, buried by almost 100 years of blowing and drifting snow, and has shifted about 3,000 feet, its exact whereabouts unknown.

Four Norwegians were headed to the Pole by snowmobile to search in 1994, but ran into a field of crevasses, many of them concealed by snow. They reportedly drove four snowmobiles at high speed into the crevasse field in a line-abreast formation, a sure invitation to disaster. Team members fell dozens of feet and had to be rescued by a joint American-New Zealand team. The leader, a thirty-five-year-old Norwegian Army captain, fell 128 feet and subsequently died, wedged inside an icy tomb at minus forty degrees Fahrenheit. The National Science Foundation was up in arms, complaining that bailing out expeditions was starting to have a detrimental effect on legitimate scientific research.

Still interested? You'll first have to receive permission from the signatories of the Antarctic Treaty to go look for it. It's a long shot indeed, so better get started if you want to do this by the 100th anniversary in 2011.

Smile for Sandy Irvine's Camera

In 1999, Bozeman, Montana, climber Conrad Anker, then thirty-six, located George Mallory's body on Mount Everest, just 2,030 feet from the summit. Mallory, who died either climbing up or descending from the summit in 1924, was known to have a Kodak camera on his expedition. It was Mallory, by the way, who is credited with the oft-quoted rationale for climbing the peak. "Because it is there," he blurted exasperatedly to a *New York Times* reporter during a preclimb press conference.

Dave Hahn, a member of the 1999 Mallory & Irvine Research Expedition, described Mallory's body in *Ghosts of Everest: The Search for Mallory & Irvine* (The Mountaineers Books, 1999): "The clothing was blasted from most of his body, and his skin was bleached white. I felt like I was viewing a Greek or Roman marble statue."

After a careful, respectful search of the body on a steep slope that could have sent any of them sliding off the edge, the team found a number of artifacts—Mallory's meat lozenges, a handkerchief monogrammed *G.L.M.*, goggles, his wristwatch, even a pocketknife with antler handle, but no camera. Could the Kodak be with Mallory's climbing partner, Andrew "Sandy" Irvine? But where are Irvine's remains? In June 1924, nearly three decades before the celebrated 1953 ascent of Everest by Sir Edmund Hillary and Tenzing Norgay, Irvine also disappeared while attempting to summit.

Mallory, thirty-seven, the premier climber of his day, and Irvine, a strapping twenty-two-year-old Oxford University rowing captain, were last seen "going strong for the top" by another member of the 1924 British Everest Expedition. Whether or not they made it before perishing is one of the most enduring mysteries in mountaineering history.

Launch an expedition to find Irvine's body and the collapsible Vest-pocket Kodak camera he is believed to have carried when they began their ascent on the morning of June 8, 1924. American researcher Tom Holzel and British historian Audrey Salkeld tried to locate the camera in 1986 and failed. Eastman Kodak scientists have researched the subject extensively and believe if the camera is found and the black and white film is intact, "printable images could result." But even if a camera is not found, it is possible that Irvine might have written about the view from the summit in a journal still in his possession.

Does it even matter whether they made it or not? Maybe not. According to *Ghosts of Everest*, "Surely what matters, what warrants our attention and our awe, is the scale of their achievement, given the resources available to them, their astonishing strength and grit, the indomitability of their desire."

Eric Simonson, co-owner of International Mountain Guides in Ashford, Washington, annually guides climbers to Mount Everest who have paid the approximately $40,000 trip cost. "When people ask about sponsorship, I encourage them to start locally, and build personal relationships with people at local companies. Some of them are successful doing this, but my question would be, 'at what cost to themselves?'"

Simonson continues, "A lot of people are under the impression that a sponsor is going to just give them money. Well, guess what? No sponsor just gives away money or product, especially in this day and age. The bottom line is someone has to pay.

"Either the individual climber pays, or the sponsor pays, and in the latter case, they get it back out of you in other respects. Once they do the calculation, I think many aspiring Everest climbers will realize that they would be better to just write the check themselves."

Want to find Irvine's camera and enter the history books? Do your homework, consult the experts, and begin training. Decide whether to pay for it yourself or seek outside funding. Professional guide services like IMG can get you to Mount Everest, but finding the camera is up to you.

Set a Record

Skydive from Space

Here's another one of those great, self-explanatory project names. But this one will take some work, a lot of money, and it certainly won't hurt if you have skydiving experience.

The record for a skydive from space has stood for almost fifty years. The world parachute jump record of 102,800 feet was set in 1960 by Colonel Joseph W. Kittinger, Jr., from Altamonte Springs, Florida. "Lord, take care of me now," he prayed as he stepped out into the void for the thirteen-minute, forty-five-second jump above New Mexico wearing nothing but a pressure suit, oxygen tank, and parachute.

In 1993, Loel P. Guinness, Jr., a wealthy member of the Guinness banking family who reportedly inherited $100 million or so, hired me to promote an attempt to break Kittinger's record with a jump by an experienced skydiver from a helium-filled balloon at 130,000 feet. Kittinger signed on as an advisor, and best-selling authors Tom Clancy and Frederick Forsyth agreed to narrate the planned live TV coverage. Accustomed to oddball adventure projects by now, I believed this one was different, not just another ill-conceived wild scheme. On the contrary, it was a well-planned and well-funded scheme to jump out of a balloon from the edge of space. Besides which, it wasn't me who was jumping.

Guinness, who bankrolled a successful Mount Everest expedition in 1989, had identified the jumper, Nish Bruce, a world-class parachutist and former member of the Red Devils—the British Army Parachute Regiment Freefall Team. The launch site was Palestine, Texas, and the entire project was falling into place until it became apparent that Guinness' Russian supplier couldn't deliver a reliable pressure suit for Nish, one that was flexible enough for him to move his arms and legs during freefall. This was rather important; if either the pressure suit or helmet leaked, unconsciousness would result in ten or twelve seconds, and death within two minutes. No jumpsuit, no jump. For this reason, and others, the Skydive from Space project was scrubbed.

"Eventually my record will be broken," Colonel Kittinger explained in 2008. "After all, that is what records are for even though in my case we were not out to set a record. We wanted to gather information for the forthcoming space program, and to provide a means of escape from high altitude."

He continued, "We accomplished both of these objectives. In fact the stabilization system that we developed over fifty years ago is still being used by air forces around the world, saving lives."

One recent attempt to break Colonel Kittinger's record was in 2008 when a misfired fuse about the size of a pen thwarted a French daredevil's third try to skydive from space. Michel Fournier's massive helium balloon launched without him one spring morning in the Canadian prairie province of Saskatchewan. According to his launch crew, a freak accident caused the equipment to strike the ground. That triggered a small explosion and separated the balloon from the capsule and its parachutes.

Fournier, sixty-four, still dreams of freefalling from 131,000 feet above the earth to break four world records in the process. The former French army colonel insists he will try again, despite the approximately $500,000 expense for a new balloon. Unless you beat him first.

Where do I want to go? During an almost forty-year career, I've traveled to every state except Mississippi. So I've got the U.S. pretty well covered.

Business has taken me to well above the Arctic Circle, to South America, plenty of places in Europe, and perhaps, someday, to the Far East.

Antarctica, however, remains my dream destination despite its reputation as the most inhospitable region of the planet. Years of watching penguin movies, sitting through PowerPoint presentations about the continent, and studying the lives of Scott, Amundsen, and Shackleton make this my number one adventure goal.

I almost managed it. In fact, my seasickness meds were purchased and my bags were packed. I had been accepted as a chaperone and writing instructor on a Students on Ice Expedition to the Antarctic peninsula. Unfortunately, twenty days before departure, on December 4, 2008, the grounding of the 278-foot *MV Ushuaia* at the entrance of Wilhelmina

Bay on the Antarctica Peninsula dashed the travel plans for me, sixty international high school students, and a team of thirty educators and chaperones participating in the trip. We were all devastated by the news, especially the twelve students awarded Students on Ice Polar Education Foundation scholarships valued at $12,500.

When the accident occurred, passengers were subsequently transferred without incident to the nearest vessel, the *MV Antarctic Dream,* located about eight miles away. Two diesel tanks were punctured, spilling a light oil which, luckily, dispersed quickly.

Writer and filmmaker Jon Bowermaster was there at the time, traveling on the *National Geographic Explorer,* another tourist ship, and blogged about the accident at jonbowermaster.com. He was quoted in the *New York Times* on December 4: "We had hurricane winds yesterday—103 miles per hour and gusting—which may have contributed to the grounding."

After reporting about the adventures of dozens of others, from amateurs to professionals like Will Steger, this was to be my trip of a lifetime. Like all good dreams, it's one that I revisit often. I am determined to eventually travel to Antarctica, just as I hope the advice in this book will help readers move at least one baby step closer to achieving their own adventure or expedition goals.

When you get there, wherever it is, whenever it is, don't forget to write.

Jeff Blumenfeld, editor
ExpeditionNews.com
editor@expeditionnews.com

🚶

Something hidden. Go and find it.
Go and look beyond the Ranges
—Something lost behind the Ranges.
Lost and waiting for you. Go!

– *The Explorer* by Rudyard Kipling, 1898

Appendix I

Target List of Adventure and Expedition Sponsors

These companies have supplied cash and/or in-kind support to adventures and expeditions in the past and may be interested in hearing about new projects.

Black Diamond (blackdiamondequipment.com)
The Coleman Company (coleman.com)
Costa del Mar (costadelmar.com)
Deuter (deuterusa.com)
Ex Officio (exofficio.com)
Helly Hansen (hellyhansen.com)
JanSport (jansport.com)
LEKI USA (leki.com)
Marmot (marmot.com)
Mountain Hard Wear (mountainhardwear.com)
The North Face (thenorthface.com)
OR (outdoorresearch.com)
Patagonia (Patagonia.com)
Rolex (rolex.com)

APPENDIX II
Adventure and Expedition Grant Programs

There's gold in them thar hills—discover the support just waiting for you. Here's a look at expedition grants available to worthy adventurers and explorers. If you're in need of money—and frankly, who isn't?—consider these funding sources.

☞ American Alpine Club

The Club's grants program awards over $50,000 annually to cutting-edge climbing expeditions, research projects, humanitarian efforts, and conservation programs. They include:

- **AAC Research Grants**—AAC Research Grants typically range from $500 to $2,000 and are given annually as a means for researchers to obtain critical seed funding to help secure sustainable funding opportunities. In 2008, twelve individuals were selected and a total of nearly $10,000 was awarded through various funds. Proposals varied from study of the effects of atmospheric nitrogen deposition on alpine lakes to arterial oxygen saturation as a predictor of next-day acute mountain sickness (americanalpineclub.org).

- **Mountain Fellowship Grants**—Since 1966, The American Alpine Club has encouraged young American climbers age twenty-five and younger to seek remote climbs more difficult than they might ordinarily be able to attempt. Any unexplored mountain ranges, unclimbed peaks, and difficult new routes are looked upon with favor, as is any project in keeping with the charter and purpose of the Club. In 2008, five climbers with an average age of twenty-two received a total of $3,900 in funding for trips around the world (americanalpineclub.org).

☞ Banff Centre for Mountain Culture Grant

The Banff Mountain Grants Program supports projects that communicate the stories of mountain landscapes as places of ecological, inspirational, and cultural value, and that celebrate the spirit of adventure. Grant officials say the communications portion has to be central to the project—not "well maybe when I get home I'll go on the road with some slides." Individuals or organizations may apply for grants of up to $5,000 (Canadian) to fund projects that creatively interpret the environment, natural history, human heritage, arts, philosophy, lifestyle, and adventure in and of the mountains. Projects must include a communications component (such as film, literature, photography) that brings the project before a public audience (banffcentre.ca).

☞ Charles A. and Anne Morrow Lindbergh Foundation

Each year, the Charles A. and Anne Morrow Lindbergh Foundation provides grants of up to $10,580 (a symbolic amount representing the cost of the *Spirit of St. Louis*) to men and women whose individual initiative and work in a wide spectrum of disciplines furthers the Lindberghs' vision of a balance between the advance of technology and the preservation of the natural human environment (lindberghfoundation.org).

☞ Earth and Space Foundation Award

In Mexico, a caving expedition studies human performance in extreme environments to improve astronaut selection. In the Sudan, an expedition uses remote sensing from satellites to study savannah flood plains to improve the productivity of rice crops. In Antarctica, researchers study microorganisms in ice and snow to try to understand possible habitats for life in cold extraterrestrial environments. Since 1994, these and other projects have been honored by Earth and Space Awards that have helped deepen the mutually beneficial connections between environmentalism and the exploration of space. The Foundation offers five Earth and Space Awards each year to expeditions that further the vision of "the earth as an oasis cared for by a space-faring civilization." Awards are approximately $500 each (earthandspace.org).

☞ The Explorers Club

The Explorers Club offers a number of grant programs as part of its public service commitment. Applications are judged on the scientific and practical merits of the proposal, the competency of the investigator, and the proposed budget. One need not be a member to apply.

- **The Explorers Club Exploration Fund**

    The Exploration Fund provides grants to graduate and postgraduate students in support of exploration and field research in amounts up to $1,500. Grants consist of direct financial support or the arrangement of opportunities to take part in expeditions under the guidance of noted explorer-scientists during the summer months.

- **The Explorers Club Youth Activities Fund**

    This fund was established to help foster a new generation of explorers and to build a reservoir of young men and women dedicated to the advancement of knowledge of the world. The Club's Youth Activities Fund is aimed at high school and college students for fieldwork conducted anywhere in the world. Awards typically range from $500 to $1,500.

    In 2008, the Club awarded three winners from each fund a total of $5,000 for projects focusing on biodiversity research and exploration; terrestrial–land-based research and exploration; and marine research and exploration.

Special grants are often issued by regional chapters for research projects funded by regions or by specific donors (explorers.org).

☞ Hans Saari Memorial Fund Exploration Grant (HSMF)

The HSMF Exploration Grant offers ski mountaineers an opportunity to receive grants for projects that expand the realm of ski mountaineering through technically challenging routes or uniquely inspirational exploration. Recipients are individuals whose goals reflect the belief that mountains are an integral part of the lives of the people who live amongst them and that physical achievement is only one component of the ski mountaineering experience. In 2008, four grants totaling $15,000 were awarded for expeditions to the Kamchatka Peninsula, Alaska's Tordrillo Mountains, and the Caucasus Range straddling the Republic of Georgia and Russia. The award was established in 2001, following the death of Hans Saari, a renowned writer and adventure columnist who was highly regarded for his ski expeditions, many of which yielded first descents of some the world's most challenging peaks (hansfund.org).

☞ Journey of a Lifetime Award

This one seems tailor-made to readers of this book. A £4,000 travel budget is available for an original and challenging journey to result in a documentary for BBC Radio 4. The aim of the award is to promote global understanding. The journey planned must be interesting and original enough to form the content of a BBC radio documentary (rgs.org/grants).

☞ Land Rover "Go Beyond" Bursary

Run by the Royal Geographical Society on behalf of Land Rover, this award provides £10,000 funding and the use of a 110 Defender vehicle to help the successful participants "go beyond" when exploring their understanding of a particular geographical concept. The loan of a vehicle must be essential to the journey and you'll need a UK driver's license (rgs.org/grants).

☞ Polartec Challenge Grant

The $10,000 Polartec International Challenge Grant has supported over 100 expeditions and adventures to every corner of the earth. It seeks to assist frugal, low-impact teams who respect the local culture and environment, and who serve as role models to outdoor enthusiasts worldwide. Applications are evaluated on the basis of their vision, commitment, and credibility. Prior winners have explored mountains, forests, caves, rivers, oceans, and deserts around the globe by nearly every means imaginable. Past recipients include outdoor pioneers and adventurers such as Conrad Anker, Jimmy Chin, Steve House, Andrew McLean, Marko Prezelj, and John Shipton. As an added bonus, in addition to grant money, winners will also be fully decked out with Polartec garments (polartec.com).

☞ Mugs Stump Award

Mugs Stump was one of North America's most prolific and imaginative climbers until his death in a crevasse fall in Alaska in May 1992. The Mugs Stump Award has helped committed climbers fulfill their dreams of fast, lightweight ascents in the world's high places since 1993. Proposed climbs should present an outstanding challenge—a first ascent, significant repeat, or first alpine-style ascent—with special emphasis placed on climbers leaving no trace of their passage. Teams and individuals from North America are eligible. You don't have to be famous, and both men and women are encouraged to apply. If you share Mugs' vision of climbing as a celebration of boldness, purity, and simplicity, and have the determination to bring your dream to life, this award can help make it happen (mugsstumpaward.com).

☞ National Geographic Expeditions Council

This grant program is dedicated to funding exploration of largely unrecorded or little-known areas of the earth, as well as regions undergoing significant environmental or cultural change. EC grants support a wide range of projects including marine research, archaeological discoveries, documentation of vanishing rain forests, first ascents, and more. The program is editorially driven; projects must have the potential for a compelling written and visual record in order for a grant to be awarded. Applications are also judged on the qualifications of applicants and their teams, and on the merit and uniqueness of the project. Grants generally range from $5,000 to $35,000 (nationalgeographic.com/council).

☞ Rolex Awards for Enterprise

The Rolex Awards for Enterprise provide visionary men and women with the financial support and recognition needed to carry out innovative projects. Awards are presented every two years and focus on improving the planet and the human condition. Categories include Exploration and Discovery, and the Environment. In 2010, five young Laureates (aged eighteen to thirty) will be selected; in 2012, five Laureates and five Associate Laureates will be chosen from among applicants of any age, nationality, or background. Young Laureate candidates cannot apply; they must be nominated by individuals or institutions selected by Rolex. Laureates receive cash prizes and Rolex chronometers. To win, projects must be original, breaking new ground in a creative and innovative manner (rolexawards.com)

☞ Waterman Fund Alpine Essay Contest

Brush up on your writing skills. The Waterman Fund seeks essays about the mountains of the northeastern U.S. for its second annual Waterman Fund Alpine Essay Contest. Stories must explore the relationship between the human spirit and the environment. Of particular interest are personal essays about stewardship of wild places, whether through a scientific lens or an encounter with wilderness. The winning story will be published in *Appalachia* journal, and the winning essayist will be awarded $2,000 (watermanfund.org).

☞ W.L. Gore Shipton/Tilman Grant

Eric Shipton and Bill Tilman were arguably the greatest adventurers of this past century. Their exploits are a catalog of bold and inspirational achievements, and have inspired many to act on their own dreams.

For years, W. L. Gore & Associates Inc., inventor of Gore-Tex fabric, has funded a total of $30,000 to be divided among three to six endeavors each year that are most in harmony with the philosophies of the grant's namesakes. Judges look for projects that use a simple and light expeditionary style. Recipients may be asked to test one of the company's new Gore products and submit an evaluation of its performance (gore-tex .com).

APPENDIX III

Memo to Sponsors: How Adventure Marketing Can Break Through the Clutter

The following is an open memo to corporate marketing executives who must decide between yet another golf or tennis sponsorship, or the next great adventure expedition project.

TO: Potential Sponsor

FROM: Jeff Blumenfeld, president, Blumenfeld and Associates, Inc., PR

RE: Break Through the Clutter with Adventure Marketing

Consider the typical golf or tennis sponsorship: the savvy marketer can sample products, entertain customers, present his latest advertising campaigns over a gourmet, alcohol-infused lunch or dinner, and distribute goodie bags brimming with imprinted polo shirts, ball caps, stress balls, and other swag. Traditional sports sponsorship is a no brainer—a slam-dunk.

But occasionally, a sponsorship opportunity arises that steps outside the box, way outside. To the ends of the earth, in fact. It takes some corporate fortitude to sponsor a mountain climbing expedition by a blind climber, an Antarctic crossing by two women, a freedive to 500-plus feet on a single breath of air, or circumnavigation of the globe by hot air balloon.

Yet if planned correctly, these adventure marketing projects can yield substantial returns: blind climber Erik Weihenmayer lands on the cover of *Time* magazine after climbing Mount Everest, generating exposure for Allegra in the process; polar explorers Ann Bancroft and Liv Arnesen capture visual identification for Volvo, Pfizer, and Motorola during an interview on *The Today Show*; and Dr. Bertrand Piccard and Brian Jones land the *Breitling Orbiter 3* balloon—named for their watch sponsor—on the cover of nearly every daily newspaper on the planet.

Sure, it's difficult to entertain customers at Everest base camp, even more so at the South Pole, but adventure marketing opportunities have their own unique set of advantages:

- For makers of outdoor gear and clothing, energy supplements, automobiles, high-tech communications equipment, and a host of other products and services, adventures and expeditions provide an opportunity to demonstrate product performance in dire conditions. These projects bestow the adventure version of the Good Housekeeping Seal of Approval. If that waterproof breathable laminate works on top of the world, the thinking goes, it will likely perform well for average human beings en route to the local grocery store.

- The public has an insatiable appetite for well-told adventure stories; consider *The Perfect Storm*, *Into Thin Air*, and the movies, books, and museum exhibitions surrounding Sir Ernest Shackleton. A sponsored explorer can tour the country for years presenting talks and PowerPoints, conducting retail sales clinics, visiting company factories, and attending trade shows. Dr. Beck Weathers almost froze to death on Mount Everest in 1996, yet he retells his tale at corporate meetings. His is a story of inspiration and survival that leaves an audience spellbound.

- Adventure marketing is cost-efficient. For typically $25,000–$100,000, expedition sponsors can receive exposure in major print and electronic media valued at two to three times their investment, or more. Some adventurers and explorers offer even greater value by accepting a combination of cash and in-kind products and services.

Years ago, the apocryphal reason for deciding what to sponsor was based on the CEO's personal interests. Golf, for instance. That policy doesn't fly any longer. In today's difficult and competitive business environment, it's vitally important to establish sponsorship-selection criteria, especially when presented with nontraditional adventure opportunities where a positive outcome is far from guaranteed.

Consider these criteria when evaluating an opportunity:

1. **Does It Answer the "So What?" Rule—Is It Newsworthy?—** Everest was first summited in 1953. What is this climber proposing to do differently, and will anyone care? Why sponsor the journey of a replica Viking ship from Iceland to New York City? Because it's the 1,000th anniversary of Leif Eriksson's discovery of the New World (and the ship sailing past the Statue of Liberty makes a great photo).

2. **Can You Become Lead Dog?—**If publicity is a main sponsorship objective, as it usually is, sponsors need to protect their position, negotiating for strong visual ID—on the front of red parkas, tents, hats, and packs that will likely appear in photo or video coverage. If that logo doesn't read from a distance, it should be redesigned in bolder fonts no smaller than six square inches for apparel, and four to five square feet for banners.

3. **Does the Explorer Have What It Takes?—**Consider experience and track record. Texas swimmer Benoit "Ben" Lecomte called

us once to pitch his attempt to swim the Pacific. "What makes you qualified to safely swim the Pacific?" we asked. His reply was impressive: "I just swam the Atlantic."

4. **What Are the Odds of Success?**—If the definition of success or failure hinges upon a single achievement—the first-ever live sighting of the giant squid, for instance—consider ways to create news even if the team fails to make a discovery. Front-load the PR campaign to generate as much preexpedition exposure as possible. Remember when TV news personality Geraldo Rivera opened Al Capone's vault in 1986? There was nothing there but some old bottles when they finally broke through the wall on live television. But the advance hype was priceless.

5. **Consider Product Integration**—Is the sponsor's product an integral part of the expedition? It should be as important as another team member. Science Diet dog food fueled a North Pole dogsled expedition; Du Pont sleeping-bag insulation protected Antarctic explorers; and Allegra, an allergy medication alleviated symptoms for Erik Weihenmayer, the blind Everest climber.

6. **Negotiate for Rights to Images**—Maintain photo and video rights on at least a shared basis with the explorer. As sponsors, you'll want unlimited use of images for publicity, advertising, newsletters, annual reports, and corporate Web sites. And while you're at it, provide the explorer with a suggested photo shot list—if they forget to photograph your banner on the summit, it's tough to go back.

Other issues to resolve well in advance of your trip include liability coverage, a specific number of appearance days, category exclusivity, payment schedules that are contingent upon reaching certain milestones, and termination clauses.

Placing a sponsor logo on a dogsled is a bit more complicated than buying signing rights to the umbrellas at a celebrity golf tournament. But with proper planning, and some due diligence, adventure sponsorships can yield a mountain of positive exposure.

**Venturing into the "Heart of Darkness": Expeditions,
Machiavelli, and a Survival Guide to Sponsorships**
by William F. Vartorella, PhD, CBC

As in most things, Niccolò Machiavelli was prescient:

"The one who adapts his policy to the times prospers, and likewise that the one whose policy clashes with the demands of the times does not."

Such is the case with the uncharted and fractious global economy and what it portends for expedition sponsorships. Sponsors, like governments, tend to take a long view. Restriction of sponsor spending is less a function of today's economy than what occurs in 2010 and beyond. Moreover, sponsors who are desperate for exit strategies from high-profile "excesses," such as skyboxes at sporting functions, are exploring exotic barter deals that can entrench their brands more economically. When you add essential, near recession-proof industries into the mix (your home's electricity provider or preferred gasoline brand), the case for expedition sponsorships is less bleak, less draconian. That bodes well for the nearly 7,000 expeditions worldwide poised to go into the field each year. Unfortunately, many are suffering from the same sponsor/donor fatigue plaguing nonprofits generally and nonessential scientific inquiry specifically.

"Bwana," clad in short pants and a pith helmet, slashing vines in darkest, darkest "wherever" is hardly the image sought by today's modern sponsor. It evokes memories of spread-eagle imperialism—the last thing the sponsor wants consumers in Timbuktu or the Ural Mountains to envision. No, the Captains of Industry see sponsorships as about "hearts and minds," geodemography, *real politik*, Machiavelli, and high-stakes market share. As per *del Principe*, one must consider "whether a prince has a state of such resources as will enable him to stand on his own feet in case of need or whether he must always have the assistance of others." For expeditions, therein lies the rub.

Sponsorships are not altruistic in intent. Their goal is the achievement of commercial objectives. For an expedition to stand above the fray in tough economic times, it must view a sponsor as an active *partner*. The talking points are brand-related—visibility, creation/change, niche specific—and must relate to consumerism, supply chain, or business-to-business (B2B).

Simply, a sponsorship is a cash or in-kind fee paid in return for access to whatever commercial potential a company believes is associated with the expedition's image, objectives, technology, and—especially—"fan" base. Best guesses place 30 percent of companies allocating perhaps 20 percent of their marketing budgets to sponsorship (perhaps $60 billion annually), as opposed to more traditional sales and communications tools. While sports remains the major focus, there is still money available for serious expeditions. To negotiate with the new princes in the new economy, remember this:

1. The market is global/local, driven by lifestyle geodemographics, experiences, and emotion. In a virtual sense, the public must share the balloon, space plane, underseas rover, or the rainforest with you. Your expedition is *not* a sponsor billboard. It's an educational experience for consumers targeted by a sponsor. Old economy: sponsor was focus. New economy: consumer is king, and the princes know it.

2. Your expedition is only as strong as its trademark(s) and brand equity. They embody your "merchantability" and can be leveraged into serious sponsorship deals through cobranding.

You, like corporate sponsors, are driven by a Mission/Vision Statement that defines you as much as the discovery of some lost city, skirting the edge of space, or coming face-to-face with some denizen from the deep.

3. Your #1 priority is getting a media sponsor early. It is a magnet for other sponsors, as it guarantees their exposure. While major market newspapers and some magazine sectors are in jeopardy, think "New Media" and the shake-out/consolidation in cellular providers. This positions your expedition for the much sought after younger adult and "tween" markets. It also positions you nicely for the hot spot in financial services—credit unions (read: the 25–45 age bracket, which is primetime for borrowing money for big-ticket items such as homes and vehicles). Tie in "green" goods and services, and you have the expedition anchors—the media, financial, coming-of-age youth products, high-profile, "earth friendly."

4. The supply chain/web of sponsors is your untapped funding pool. B2B linkages are profitable alliances. The more high-tech your expedition, the more deeply you should explore B2B corporate donors, especially in Asia. In some developing regions, 10,000 brands compete head-to-head with global brands. The locals are key targets, especially for in-kind support. Identify the brands in-country, create a "grid" of who, where, how much, and why, and initiate open discussions with the global subsidiaries or the locally-entrenched brands.

5. Public interactivity is crucial to expedition sponsorships. Web cams are common; move into podcasting, interactive texting, and blogging. Exploit the youth market, and sponsors will salivate. Follow the analog of Lenovo computers and the Olympics. In a soft market for computers, Lenovo lever-

aged "social media," connectivity, and blogs to raise consumer awareness *indirectly* and efficiently. When your expedition thinks "technology," think seamless, connected, social, viral, and—especially—measurable.

6. The true technology demonstrator and cobranding marketplace is the Internet. The "capture" of email addresses, with permission, and a posted explanation of how they will be used by sponsors in exchange for prizes, discount offers, and other considerations, is a critical strategy. Create a consumer database for sponsors. This "product advantage" distinguishes you from competing expeditions.

7. The interface for the natural, built, and human environments blur as expeditions become more environmentally "green" and adopt a Mission Statement with philanthropic goals and objectives to help local communities attain sustainable futures.

8. Social conscience equals good business. Adopt a local NGO (non-governmental organization). Help it raise money.

9. Specialist expeditions will evolve to exploit specific sponsor goals and objectives within discrete markets. These "hired guns" will bring high-profile explorers, team, interactive Web site, and marketing and hospitality personnel to a project with a plan of brand enrichment for the "client" and its supply chain. An example is the polar bear—a sentry species and poster child for global warming. Polar bears as brand logos are ubiquitous—from sweets to bottled waters to alcoholic beverages, etc. Excellent opportunity for cobranding for the right Arctic expedition. Similar opportunities exist for Egyptology, with "borrowed interest" imagery used by brands ranging from beer and distilled spirits to airlines, casinos, and

Hollywood studios. Again, look at product lines that tend to be recession-resistant/proof.

10. Measure success in consumer, as well as expedition, terms. New consumer lists for sponsors. New "lost" cities discovered. Consumer is #1, Sponsor is #2, Expedition is #3. Think in terms of "value added," "bonus circulation" to sponsors. And a final "killer app": ask for mentoring first (advice and infrastructure), in-kind contributions second (GPS, satellite telephone and air time, petrol in the bush, discounted airfares or matching of frequent-flyer miles, etc.) and cash— last. Structure the cash infusion in comfortable stages with clear benchmarks. "Sit down, don't talk down." Sponsors are people. People give money to people, not to ideas.

Someone once wrote, "adventure is the result of poor planning." Sponsors don't like surprises. The boardroom is no place for tales from the crypt.

William F. Vartorella, PhD, CBC, is the coauthor (with Don Keel) of Funding Exploration: the Challenge and Opportunity for Funding Science and Discovery in the 21st Century *(Marco Polo Monographs #9, 2004). He is a Fellow of The Explorers Club and The Royal Geographical Society. Vartorella has expedition field experience in the U.K., Middle East, South America, and the U.S. He was a co–expedition leader on the successful retrieval of the Lake Murray B-25C Bomber and negotiated the expedition's media deal with the television production company that documented the event for the* History Channel's Mega-Movers *series. His firm is an associate sponsor of a winning, electric open-wheel racecar.*

Vartorella lectures worldwide on the theme of "sustainable futures" for science and exploration and can be reached at (803) 432-4353 or globebiz@camden.net.

APPENDIX V

Ten Tips for Negotiating Expedition Sponsorship
by David G. Concannon, Esq.

Exploration is fraught with peril. Explorers encounter danger not only on expeditions, but they must also successfully negotiate a myriad of issues just to get their expeditions into the field. One such issue is negotiating expedition sponsorship. Expeditions cost a lot of money. In fact, many expeditions would never get beyond the dream stage if it were not for the support of generous corporate benefactors. To help explorers achieve their dreams, here are ten tips for negotiating expedition sponsorship.

1. Consult a Good Attorney

Remember, where explorers go, lawyers follow. You may be good at handling expedition logistics, but you will never be able to successfully negotiate expedition sponsorship unless you know the business of exploration. You need a good attorney. Find a lawyer who is experienced in the business of exploration, including the licensing of photographic and video rights, determining the value of the project, and legal issues related to the Internet and liability. Your lawyer should also have experience participating in expeditions in the field. If the attorney understands your business from personal experience, he or she will be better able to represent your interests. Although the thought of needing an attorney before you leave for an expedition may be unpleasant, it is less painful than dealing with an attorney after something goes wrong in the field. A good attorney who is familiar with the business of exploration can help you foresee problems before they arise. Having an attorney on your side will also level the playing field, since corporate sponsors will almost certainly be represented by counsel in conducting their negotiations.

2. Understand Your Legal Rights and Responsibilities

Even though you should be represented by a good attorney, it helps if you understand your legal rights and responsibilities. Every corporate sponsorship agreement will have provisions for indemnification, performance obligations, and payment. These provisions should be fair to both sides. You need to understand what is expected of you so you can let your lawyer and the sponsor know what you can and cannot do. Don't make promises you cannot keep.

3. Understand Intellectual Property Rights

Intellectual property rights include copyrights, trademarks, photographic and video rights, and rights of publicity. These are valuable assets that should not be overlooked. In fact, many expeditions are substantially or completely underwritten by the sale or licensing of video and photographic rights. It is essential for you to know what intellectual property rights you have and what they may be worth.

4. Know How Much Sponsorship You Need

One of the most common problems explorers face in negotiating corporate sponsorship is knowing exactly how much their expeditions will cost, and therefore how much sponsorship they will actually need. This is especially true where the expedition is venturing into uncharted territory. Resist the urge to under-budget your needs. Instead, put together a realistic assessment of what the expedition could cost and plan accordingly.

5. Consider In-Kind Contributions

When budgeting for an expedition, first put together a list of what the expedition could cost if all of the equipment, transportation, supplies, services, and other logistical components were paid for in cash. Then identify which components could be obtained through in-kind contributions. Many companies will donate equipment in exchange for an endorsement, publicity for their product, or the chance to test it in the field. Moreover, it may be cheaper or easier for a company to donate equipment or services instead of cash. You can substantially reduce the total cost of your expedition by obtaining in-kind contributions.

6. Know What Type of Sponsorship to Seek

When you have a realistic assessment of what your expedition is worth, you can begin to identify potential corporate sponsors. Be creative. You never know who may be interested in helping you achieve your goals. Equipment manufacturers may get thousands of requests for sponsorship each year, but food manufacturers or telecommunications companies may not get any. Identify each potential sponsor's target market and determine how your expedition will help the sponsor achieve its marketing goals. Then pitch the potential sponsor by showing how your expedition will fulfill their objectives as well as your own.

7. Know What Other Expeditions Are Getting

One way to determine the worth of your expedition is to know what type of sponsorship other expeditions are getting. Are similar expeditions getting equipment donations? If so, what kind? Were they able to sell or license their video or photographic rights? If so, how much did they get? By answering these questions, you can determine how much corporate sponsorship to expect for your expedition and where to look for it.

8. Consider Incorporating Your Expedition

Incorporating your expedition as a legal entity provides you with protection from personal liability as well as other benefits. If possible, you should consider incorporating your expedition as a nonprofit organization under either federal or state law. This provides the added convenience of allowing your corporate sponsors to take a tax deduction for their contributions to the expedition.

9. Maximize the Potential of the Internet

The explosion of the Internet has dramatically changed the field of exploration. The Internet can be the most lucrative avenue to corporate sponsorship, but it is often the most overlooked. Proper use of the Internet ensures maximum exposure for you and your sponsors. However, the Internet carries special legal considerations, such as the propriety of linking between commercial and nonprofit sites, copyright and trademark protection, and properly evaluating the value of corporate sponsorship and electronic media rights. This area of the law changes rapidly, so it deserves special attention.

10. It Is Never Too Late to Obtain Corporate Sponsorship

If you want to be a successful explorer, you can never stop marketing yourself or your expeditions. You should seek corporate sponsors before, during, and after your expedition. It's never too late to obtain corporate sponsorship, even if it's for the next expedition after this one.

David G. Concannon, Esq., is the founder of Explorer Consulting LLC, in Wayne, Pennsylvania. Concannon is a Fellow of The Explorers Club and the former chairman of its legal committee. He has been a legal advisor to two Everest expeditions, six Titanic expeditions, and several other international expeditions. He served as General Counsel to the X-Prize Foundation when it awarded $10 million for the first private space flights, and to a variety of organizations involved in exploration. An accomplished explorer, Concannon has climbed to 17,000 feet, and made four submersible dives to the Titanic, at a depth of 12,500 feet, and a submersible dive to one of the world's deepest shipwrecks, at a depth of 16,109 feet. Concannon can be reached at (610) 293-8084 or concannonlaw@msn.com.

APPENDIX VI

Picture Perfect: 10 Tips to Take Better Expedition Photos
By Jake Norton

It's happened to all of us. You go on the trip of a lifetime—Mount Rainier, Peru, the Himalayas—and take loads of images. You get home, look at those images, but the mystery, the magic of the place, is missing. What went wrong? Where did all those great vistas, enthralling clouds, and stunning sunsets go? These ten simple tips will help you take your expedition images to the next level.

1. The Rule of Thirds

Divide your frame into thirds, both vertically and horizontally, and place your main subject where those lines intersect rather than in the middle. This helps create energy and movement in the image and a dynamic and engaging composition.

2. Leapfrog!

Let's face it—butt shots just don't work. As long as it's safe, leapfrog your climbing partners, or shoot the rope team behind—getting their faces—rather than the behinds of the team ahead.

3. More Isn't Always Better

Use a zoom lens to pull an interesting subject more fully into the frame . . . or, use that old tried and true tool—your legs. Yup, that's right, if your lens can't do it, move closer, compose and shoot. It's all in the perspective.

4. Panorama

Shoot multiple frames of a dramatic vista, overlapping the edges of each image by at least 25 percent. Later on, use a panorama stitching program (like Adobe Photoshop's built-in Photomerge function) to put the images together—works like a charm!

5. Have Camera...Will Get Shot

Sounds simple, but you'd be amazed by how often people either leave their camera behind—and of course miss images—or have it tucked so far out of reach that it is too tough (or too dangerous) to get it out when that perfect moment arises. Keep it on you and keep it handy.

6. Stop It Down

High contrast scenes—like mountainscapes—tend to trick even modern cameras, resulting in loss of detail in the highlights. The solution is to manually under-expose the image by ⅓ to ⅔ of a stop. Lock in this setting on your camera and shoot in any shooting mode, and your photos will come out with details in the highlights (snow) while still being good in the darker areas.

7. Fill 'Er Up

Dark subject on a bright background? Use a little bit of fill-flash, stopped down to -0.7 to -1.0 (⅔ to one full stop), and sometimes even more depending on the situation.

8. Sun Star

Make the sun pop by setting your aperture to f16 or above. Then set the exposure ½ to 1½ stops under-exposed. Shoot a frame and make sure the sun is as starred as you want it to be while the rest of your image has proper exposure as well.

9. Zoom In or Pull Back

As I mentioned earlier, perspective is everything. So, try different perspectives both by using your legs to move around and by using different lenses to change the view. Zoom in close or go super-wide to bring everything in. Lie down on the ground and shoot skyward, or climb up a bit higher and shoot a bird's eye view.

10. Try Some of Everything

Although equipment today is amazing, the best photographs require a combination of equipment and personal vision. Rarely does a simple point-and-shoot image make the cover of *National Geographic*. So, try a little bit of everything on your next outing or expedition. Have fun, play around. Figure out what the story is you want to tell, and then decide what images will best tell that story. The best shot is sometimes the one you decided not to take.

Jake Norton is a professional climber, photographer, and motivational speaker. For more advice log onto mountainworld.typepad.com or mountainworldproductions.com.

APPENDIX VII

Favorite Adventure Books

Before you set out on your own adventure or expedition, become a student of those who have gone before. Here are some of my favorite books on the subject:

Adventures of Huckleberry Finn—Mark Twain (1884). The classic American novel that inspired countless budding adventurers. "Huck's always been my hero," polar explorer Will Steger says. "I've patterned my life after his."

Annapurna—Maurice Herzog (The Lyons Press, paperback edition, 1997). French climber Maurice Herzog's gripping and horrific account of the first ascent of an 8,000-meter peak in 1950.

Arctic Dreams—Barry Lopez (Charles Scribner's Sons, 1986). An inspiring, classic celebration of the Arctic region.

The Brotherhood of the Rope: The Biography of Charles Houston—Bernadette McDonald (The Mountaineers Books, 2007). The story of the 1953 K2 expedition and the famed belay that saved five people.

Crossing Antarctica—Will Steger and Jon Bowermaster (Alfred A. Knopf, 1991). First-person account of the $11 million expedition that will be remembered as both Antarctica's final dogsled adventure and the longest of any kind ever.

Endurance: Shackleton's Incredible Voyage—Alfred Lansing (The Adventure Library, 1994 Edition). One of the greatest rescue stories ever told.

Eric Shipton: Everest & Beyond—Peter Steele (The Mountaineers Books, 1998). An in-depth look at this climbing and exploration legend who explored at a time when there were still white spaces on the map.

Into Thin Air—Jon Krakauer (Villard Books, 1997)—Hard to believe, but climbing Everest became even more popular after the 1996 tragedy was recounted in such vivid detail.

Kon Tiki—Thor Heyerdahl (Rand McNally & Company, 1950). "Fishing was easy; sometimes the bonitos swam aboard with the waves." Feel the romance of one of the world's best-known expeditions by reading an original edition purchased from a used book store.

The Last Climb: The Legendary Everest Expeditions of George Mallory— David Breashears and Audrey Salkeld (National Geographic, 1999). Did Mallory and Irvine reach the summit? Where's Irvine's camera? Better read this if you have any hopes of finding it on your own expedition.

The Last Step: The American Ascent of K2—Rick Ridgeway (The Mountaineers Books, 1980). What can go wrong on an expedition? Plenty. This is a first-person account of a K2 climb, warts and all.

North to the Pole—Will Steger with Paul Schurke (Times Books, 1987). Could Robert E. Peary have reached the North Pole in 1909 unsupported? Will and Paul demonstrate in fifty-five days and a thousand zigzag miles how it could have been done.

Sea of Glory—Nathaniel Philbrick (Viking, 2003). Lewis and Clark got all the publicity thirty years before, but the U.S. Exploring Expedition of 1838 to 1842 was the granddaddy of American seagoing expeditions.

Shackleton—Roland Huntford (Ballantine, 1987). The definitive Shackleton, every excruciating moment of his extraordinary life.

Snowstruck: In the Grip of Avalanches—Jill Fredston (Harcourt, 2005). Fredston is one of North America's leading avalanche experts. Dreaming of a white Christmas? Read this and you'll think of snow in a whole new light.

Surviving the Extremes: A Doctor's Journey to the Limits of Human Endurance—Kenneth Kamler, MD (St. Martin's Press, 2004). This expedition doctor has seen it all. You will reconsider swimming in an Amazon lakes after reading about the candiru.

The Seven Summits—Dick Bass and Frank Wells with Rick Ridgeway (Warner Books, Inc., 1986). Two middle-aged men with a dream to be first to climb the highest mountain on each of the seven continents. The Seven Summits craze started here.

They Lived to Tell the Tale: True Stories of Modern Adventure from the Legendary Explorers Club—Jan Jarboe Russell, editor (The Lyons Press, 2008).Oceanographers, naturalists, Arctic explorers, NASA astronauts, and even an ethnobotanist all recount their most memorable projects.

Touch the Top of the World—Erik Weihenmayer (Penguin Putnam, 2001). The story of the first blind climber to summit Mount Everest. His guide dog was a chick magnet, but can he really tell the denomination of paper bills by smell alone?

APPENDIX VIII

Reference Books

Climbing: Training for Peak Performance—Clyde Soles (The Mountaineers Books, 2008). Focuses on how to prepare for an expedition, including the importance of diet and exercise.

Climbing: Expedition Planning—Clyde Soles and Phil Powers (The Mountaineers Books, 2003). A guide for intermediate to advanced climbers who want to broaden their experience in other parts of the globe and break out from guided climbs to venture out on their own.

Expedition Medicine—David Warrell and Sarah Anderson (editors) (Profile Books, 2002). Advice and information on first-aid kits, emergency evacuation procedures, and health advice for a wide range of environments and activities from the tropics to the polar regions, and from mountaineering to diving and canoeing.

Mountaineering: The Freedom of the Hills—Steven M. Cox and Kris Fulsaas (editors) (The Mountaineers Books, 2003). The climber's bible, an essential mountaineering reference.

Royal Geographical Society Expedition Handbook—Shane Winser, editor (Profile Books, 2004). Assisting expeditions since 1830, the RGS knows a thing or two about planning and fund-raising, including why divers shouldn't wear gloves, why sharpening machetes can affect navigation in the rainforest, and how aluminum-foil blankets can be useful in the desert. One favorite passage about camel expeditions reads, "Camels do not spit, they vomit, and if you are standing in front of an irate animal, you may get the entire stomach contents in your face!"

APPENDIX IX

Favorite Web sites

Avalanche Information
American Institute for Avalanche Research and Education
avtraining.org

Colorado Avalanche Information Center
avalanche.state.co.us

National Snow and Ice Data Center
nsidc.org/snow/avalanche

Northwest Weather and Avalanche Center
nwac.us

Climbing
American Safe Climbing Association
safeclimbing.org

Corporate Sponsorship Resource
International Events Group (IEG)
sponsorship.com

Expedition Information
- explorersweb.com
- adventurestats.com

- adventureweather.com
- k2climb.net
- mounteverest.net
- theoceans.net
- thepoles.com

Polar Organizations

American Polar Society

ampolarsociety.org

British Antarctic Survey

antarctica.ac.uk

Shipwreck Archaeology

Institute of Nautical Archaeology (INA)

Texas A & M

nautarch.tamu.edu

Travel Web sites

Lonely Planet

lonelyplanet.com

Rough Guides

roughguides.com

Women Explorers Resource

WINGS WorldQuest

Education & Resource Center

wingsworldquest.org

APPENDIX X

Inspiring Films

These great adventure movies promise an "edge of your seat" experience that will inspire anyone who dreams of the trip of a lifetime. Netflix these before you leave:

Around the World in 80 Days (1956)—Englishman Phileas Fogg (David Niven), takes on a seemingly impossible wager: traveling around the world with his sidekick, Passepartout (Cantinflas), in eighty days. Sure, there have been remakes over the years, but this is the one many explorers grew up viewing. It makes you appreciate the late Steve Fossett's first solo balloon circumnavigation, which took him a little over thirteen days.

Encounters at the End of the World (2007)—Unforgettable images of jellyfish under Antarctica sea ice, penguins that have seemingly gone insane, and quirky interviews with National Science Foundation scientists who apparently have spent a little too much time under the ozone hole. Produced and narrated by celebrated German documentary filmmaker Werner Herzog, who also directed *Grizzly Man*.

Everest: IMAX (1998)—This is the number one IMAX film of all time (grossing over $146 million) formatted for the small screen. Filmed by David Breashears at the time of the 1996 Everest tragedy, it tells of avalanches, scarce oxygen, hazardous ice walls, and an infamous deadly snowstorm.

Journey to the Center of the Earth (1959)—No, we're not talking about the recent 3D fantasy film for kids. Go see the original with James Mason, a singing Pat Boone, and a duck named Gertrude. So what if the iguanas have fake fins glued to them?

Lost Horizon (1937)—In Frank Capra's classic based on the James Hilton novel, plane-crash survivors are led through the Himalayas to Shangri-La, a village without hate or crime, and where no one ages. The film is said to be inspired at least in part by accounts of travels in Tibetan borderlands, published in *National Geographic* magazine by the explorer and botanist Joseph Rock.

Scott of the Antarctic—(1949) A realistic look at the plight faced by Robert F. Scott during his ill-fated attempt to be first to the South Pole. It stars John Mills at his stiff-upper-lipped best.

Seven Years in Tibet (1997)—Brad Pitt portrays the life of famed Austrian mountaineer Heinrich Harrer as he journeys to the Himalayas, without his family, to head an expedition in 1939. World War II unfortunately gets in the way.

Touching the Void (2003)—Documentary based upon the book by climber Joe Simpson of a near fatal climb of a 21,000-foot mountain in the Peruvian Andes in 1985. His climbing partner cut the rope connecting the two; Simpson fell into a crevasse, yet miraculously rescued himself.

APPENDIX XI

Top-Notch Guide Services and Schools

Climbing and Mountaineering
Alaska Mountaineering School
Talkeetna, Alaska
climbalaska.org

Colorado Mountain School
Boulder, Colorado
totalclimbing.com

International Mountain Climbing School
North Conway, New Hampshire
ime-usa.com

Yosemite Mountaineering School
Yosemite National Park, California
yosemitepark.com

Climbs and Treks
Adventure Consultants
Wanaka, New Zealand
adventureconsultants.co.nz

International Mountain Guides
Ashford, Washington
mountainguides.com

Summit Climb
Lakebay, Washington
summitclimb.com

Polar Journeys
Canadian Arctic Holidays
Alcove, Quebec
canadianarcticholidays.ca

Wintergreen Dogsled Lodge Inc.
Ely, Minnesota
dogsledding.com

Wilderness Survival
Boulder Outdoor Survival School
Boulder, Colorado
boss-inc.com

ABOUT THE AUTHOR

JEFF BLUMENFELD IS FOUNDER OF BLUMENFELD AND ASSOCIATES, INC., a public relations and special-events firm based in Darien, Connecticut, that has served some of the largest outdoor recreation companies in the U.S. Clients have included Coleman, Duofold, Du Pont, Eddie Bauer, Lands' End, LEKI USA, Lewmar, Mares, Orvis, Timberland, Timex, W.L. Gore & Associates, and Wacoal Sports Science Corp.

Blumenfeld is also editor and publisher of *Expedition News*, a newsletter, blog, and Web site (expeditionnews.com) he founded in 1994 to cover news about the adventure marketing field. Excerpts from *Expedition News* also appear in The Explorers Club *Explorers Journal*.

A member of The Explorers Club in New York, he also belongs to the American Alpine Club, based in Golden, Colorado, and is a Fellow of the Royal Geographical Society in London, where he has presented talks on adventure marketing.

Blumenfeld has traveled on business to some of the remotest regions on earth. He journeyed to Anadyr, an isolated outpost in the Soviet Far East, escorted media personnel to an Eskimo village on Canada's Baffin Island; and has been to Iceland, a long-time client. A media trip to Yellowknife, NWT, for Lands' End included a dogsled trip for reporters, cross-country skiing on a frozen lake, and a spectacular display of the northern lights.

Blumenfeld journeyed to Santiago, Chile, to organize the first ski race in Antarctica, spent two weeks in Nome and Anchorage during promotion of an expedition across the Bering Strait, enlisted a team of ski instructors to test ski apparel at 12,000 feet in the High Andes of Argentina, and promoted skiing and a midnight golf tournament near the Arctic Circle in Iceland. He's co-organized media hiking trips to Salzburg, Austria, and to the summit of Snowbird, Utah, on behalf of W.L. Gore & Associates.

In 1996, after tragedy struck Mount Everest and eight people died, *LIFE* magazine hired Blumenfeld to help research their coverage of the disaster.

Blumenfeld is a former adjunct faculty member of the New York University School of Continuing and Professional Studies/Marketing and Management Institute. A graduate of Syracuse University, he holds a Bachelor of science in television and radio from the S.I. Newhouse School of Journalism. He is a board member of Voices of September 11, the leading advocacy group for the friends and families of victims of 9/11 (voicesofsept11.org), and a member of the New Canaan, Connecticut Community Emergency Response Team (CERT). An avid sea kayaker, fly-fishing angler, downhill skier, and sailor, he's also fluent in Morse code, although he'll be first to admit it doesn't come up too often in conversation.

INDEX